Heidegger's Later Philosophy

Heidegger's later philosophy has often been regarded as a lapse into unintelligible mysticism. While not ignoring its deep and difficult complexities, Julian Young's book explains in simple and straightforward language just what it is all about. It examines Heidegger's identification of loss of 'the gods', the violence of technology and humanity's 'homelessness' as symptoms of the destitution of modernity, and his notion that overcoming 'oblivion of Being' is the essence of a turning to a post-destitute, genuinely post-modern existence. Young argues that Heidegger's conception of such an overcoming is profoundly fruitful with respect to the ancient quest to discover the nature of the good life. His book will be an invaluable resource for both students and scholars of Heidegger's works.

JULIAN YOUNG is Honorary Research Associate at the University of Auckland. His publications include *Willing and Unwilling: a Study in the Philosophy of Arthur Schopenhauer* (1987), *Nietzsche's Philosophy of Art* (1992), *Heidegger, Philosophy, Nazism* (1997) and *Heidegger's Philosophy of Art* (2001).

Heidegger's Later Philosophy

Julian Young

University of Auckland

CAMBRIDGE
UNIVERSITY PRESS

CAMBRIDGE UNIVERSITY PRESS
Cambridge, New York, Melbourne, Madrid, Cape Town, Singapore, São Paulo

Cambridge University Press
The Edinburgh Building, Cambridge CB2 2RU, UK

Published in the United States of America by Cambridge University Press, New York

www.cambridge.org
Information on this title: www.cambridge.org/9780521809221

First published 2002

A catalogue record for this publication is available from the British Library

ISBN-13 978-0-521-80922-1 hardback
ISBN-10 0-521-80922-3 hardback

ISBN-13 978-0-521-00609-5 paperback
ISBN-10 0-521-00609-0 paperback

Transferred to digital printing 2006

For Christopher and Mal

Contents

Acknowledgments

I should like to thank Thomas Rohkrämer, Friedrich Voit, Jeff Malpas, Charles Guignon, Sebastian Gardner, Janny Jonkers, Anja van Polanen Petel, Kathy Crosier, Rory Spence and Christine Swanton, who, in diverse ways, have made this a better book than it would otherwise have been. My greatest debt is to Hubert Dreyfus who took a fine tooth comb through more than one version of the manuscript. (There remains much, however, with which he would certainly disagree.)

Abbreviations

AWP	'The Age of the World Picture'
QCT	'The Question concerning Technology'
SR	'Science and Reflection'
TT	'The Turning'
	all in *The Question concerning Technology and other Essays* trans. W. Lovitt (New York: Harper and Row, 1977).
BDT	'Building Dwelling Thinking'
OWA	'The Origin of the Work of Art'
PMD	'...Poetically Man dwells...'
T	'The Thing'
WPF	'What are Poets for?'
	all in *Poetry, Language, Thought* trans. A. Hofstadter (New York: Harper and Row, 1971).
ET	'On the Essence of Truth'
IWM	'Introduction to "What is Metaphysics"'
LH	'Letter on "Humanism"'
QB	'On the Question of Being'
	all in *Pathmarks* ed. W. McNeill (Cambridge: Cambridge University Press, 1998).
LS	'The call to Labour Service'
OM	'Overcoming Metaphysics'
S	'Only a God can save us': *Der Spiegel*'s interview with Martin Heidegger (1966)
	all in *The Heidegger Controversy* ed. R. Wolin (Cambridge: MIT Press, 1993).
BP	*The Basic Problems of Phenomenology* trans. A. Hofstadter (Bloomington: Indiana University Press, 1988).
BT	*Being and Time* trans. J. Macquarrie and T. Robinson (Oxford: Blackwell, 1962). Numerals refer to the pagination of the 7th German edition of *Sein und Zeit* given by Macquarrie and Robinson in the margins.

BW   *Martin Heidegger: Basic Writings* ed. D. F. Krell (San Francisco: Harper and Row, 1977).

D   *Denkerfahrungen 1910–1976* (Frankfurt-on-Main: Klostermann, 1983).

DK   '*Denken und Kunst*' in *Japan und Heidegger – Gedenkschrift der Stadt Messkirch zum hundertsten Geburtstag Martin Heideggers* (Sigmarinen: J. Thorbecke, 1989) pp. 211–15.

DL   'A Dialogue on Language' in *On the Way to Language* trans. P. Hertz (New York: Harper and Row, 1971).

DT   *Discourse on Thinking* trans. J. M. Anderson and E. H. Freund (San Francisco: Harper and Row, 1966).

E   *Erinnerung an Martin Heidegger* ed. G. Neske (Pfullingen: Neske, 1977).

GA   *Martin Heidegger: Gesamtausgabe* ed. F.-W. von Herrmann (Frankfurt-on-Main: Klostermann, 1977 and onwards). Numerals refer to volume numbers from this collected works.

HE   'Hölderlin and the Essence of Poetry' in *Existence and Being* ed. W. Brock (London: Vision, 1949) pp. 291–315.

HIC   *Martin Heidegger in Conversation* ed. R. Wisser, trans. B. S. Murthy (New Delhi: Arnold-Heinemann, 1970).

HPA   *Heidegger's Philosophy of Art* Julian Young (Cambridge: Cambridge University Press, 2000).

HPN   *Heidegger, Philosophy, Nazism* Julian Young (Cambridge: Cambridge University Press, 1997).

I   *Hölderlin's Hymn 'The Ister'* trans. W. McNeill and J. Davis (Bloomington: Indiana University Press, 1996).

ID   *Identität und Differenz* (Pfullingen: Neske, 1990).

IM   *An Introduction to Metaphysics* trans. R. Mannheim (New Haven: Yale University Press, 1959).

N   *Nietzsche*, 4 volumes, trans. D. F. Krell (San Francisco: Harper Collins 1979–82). Roman numerals refer to volume numbers.

P   *Parmenides* trans. A. Schuwer and R. Rojcewicz (Bloomington: Indiana University Press, 1992).

TB   *On Time and Being* trans. J. Stambaugh (New York: Harper and Row, 1972).

VA   *Vorträge und Aufsätze*, 3 vols. (Pfullingen: Neske, 1959).

WCT   *What is called Thinking?* trans. J. G. Gray (New York: Harper and Row, 1968).

Introduction

1. This is the final volume of my three-volume[1] attempt to understand and communicate the insights of Martin Heidegger, the thinker who seems to me, in spite of his large political error and occasional philosophical errors, the most important philosopher of modern times. Of the three volumes this is the most personal; personal in the sense that, save where I explicitly criticize him, the views I attribute to Heidegger are ones I have learnt to adopt as my own.

As its title indicates, the book is concerned with the philosophy of the later Heidegger. By 'later Heidegger' I mean, at a first approximation, the Heidegger who, by his own account made a radical 'turn' away from his earlier philosophy, the philosophy of *Being and Time* (1927), a turn that began in 1930 (LH p. 250) and completed itself during 1936–8 (GA 15 p. 366). Really, however, what I mean is 'finished' Heidegger, or, better put, the Heidegger who had progressed as far as he was to go along his 'path of thinking'. Occasionally there are respects in which that point is reached in texts which antedate the 'later' period. Hence, though most of my discussion is confined to texts written after 1936 I have not hesitated to dip, on occasion, into earlier works.

2. A common assumption, even among those well-disposed to Heidegger, is that his 'real' philosophy stops with *Being and Time*, and that what he produced after 1927 is both incomprehensible and, *qua* philosophy at least, worthless. Two factors, in particular, have encouraged this view.

The first lies in the undoubted contrast in style between early and late Heidegger. While *Being and Time*'s style, though difficult, is still, in a broad sense, 'scientific', the style adopted after the mid-1930s becomes ever more increasingly 'poetic'. This has encouraged the view that later Heidegger

---

[1] The first and second volumes are *Heidegger, Philosophy, Nazism* (Cambridge University Press, 1997), hereafter *HPN*, and *Heidegger's Philosophy of Art* (Cambridge University Press, 2000), hereafter *HPA*.

lapsed from philosophy into the (by definition) incomprehensibility of mysticism. Bernd Magnus expresses this common view when he writes that '[i]n the end' 'the author of *Being and Time* yields to mysticism'.[2]

The second factor that has encouraged the rejection of later Heidegger as philosophy is his own frequent tendency to do so; to represent himself as engaging in a new kind of post-philosophical, 'meditative' thinking.

Neither of these reasons, however, is adequate to sustain its conclusion. Though later Heidegger's writing (and hence thought) is indeed highly poetic this by no means excludes the possibility – which I shall suggest to be the truth of the matter – that it is *also* philosophical. Magnus' assumption that poetry (or 'mysticism') and philosophy are antithetical represents an old, Platonic prejudice which, as we will see, is highly suspect.

As to Heidegger's own positioning of himself after the 'end of philosophy' (a dangerous stance, since it invites over-trumping), what needs to be observed is that he does so only when he uses 'philosophy' as a synonym for what he calls 'metaphysics', a position which he regards as the most disastrous of all errors.

At other times, for example in the 1966 interview with the magazine *Der Spiegel* (S), he is perfectly happy to describe himself as doing philosophy. The conclusion is, therefore, that when he represents himself as 'after philosophy' he is really only representing himself as 'after *bad* philosophy'.

What is odd about the Heidegger admirer who holds that the real philosophy stopped in 1927 is this. *Being and Time* he regards as a great work and its author, therefore, as a great thinker. But when someone one recognizes as a great thinker calls his early work a 'dead end' (GA 15 p. 366)[3] demanding the 'reversal'[4] represented by his later thinking, then, on pain of inconsistency, one should take very seriously the idea that the great thinker's greatest thoughts are to be found in the later rather than earlier work. This is my approach and conviction.

3. In chapter 1, I outline what Heidegger (correctly) claims to be the foundation of all his thinking, his *Seinsphilosophie*, his 'philosophy of Being', a label that covers his account of truth and reality, as well as what he takes to be a

---

[2] *Heidegger's Metahistory of Philosophy* (The Hague: Nijhoff, 1970) p. 141.
[3] See, further, chapter 1, footnote 2.
[4] Heidegger's word for 'the turning' in his thinking is '*Kehre*', U-turn, rather than '*Wende*', curve.

fundamental and deeply entrenched error concerning these topics which he calls 'metaphysics'.

In chapter 2, borrowing a metaphor from Nietzsche, I view Heidegger as the 'physician' of modern Western culture. *Qua* physician, I suggest, he identifies three leading symptoms of modernity's spiritual 'sickness': loss of the gods, the 'violence' of technology, and loss of 'dwelling' or 'homelessness'.

Since Heidegger claims his philosophy of Being to be the foundation of all his thinking, it is important not to separate Heidegger the 'ontologist' (actually a bad word to apply to later Heidegger) from Heidegger the cultural critic and philosopher of technology. We must, rather, seek to discover the *unity* of his later philosophy, seek to understand how his cultural criticism and philosophy of technology are grounded in his philosophy of Being. Specifically, we must undertake the difficult task of understanding his reason for claiming that the underlying cause of each of the three symptoms of our culture's 'destitution' is the mistake about Being which he calls 'metaphysics'.

I conclude chapter 2 by asking why it is that metaphysics is the underlying ground of loss of the gods. In chapter 3 – a discussion of Heidegger's claim that the 'essence' of modernity is what he calls *Gestell* ('Enframing') – I ask the same question with respect to the alleged 'violence' of modern technology, and in chapter 4 – concerned, mainly, with death – with respect to modernity's loss of 'dwelling'.

In chapter 5, I turn from the diagnostic to the therapeutic aspect of Heidegger's 'medical' thinking, to his account of the character of 'the turning' of our culture to a new, post-'destitute', post-metaphysical, post-modern age that we must hope for, and of what we can do to promote it. The central argument of this chapter is that, in spite of his severe critique of modern technology, later Heidegger is no Luddite. Though the turning to a new age (the 'world turning', as I call it, as opposed to the 'personal turning' which might occur in the life of an individual) will represent a radical transformation of life it will not involve the breaking of machines.

In chapter 6, I canvass the commonly raised objection that (contrary to the presupposition of chapter 5) there is actually *no* therapeutic phase in Heidegger's later thinking, that according to the 'fatalism' summed up in his remark that 'only a God can save us' there is nothing at all we can do to promote the turning to a new age. In chapters 7 and 8, I prepare the ground for the rejection of this claim by looking in some detail at what it is that constitutes the life of one who has made the ('personal') turning – the turn from destitution to 'dwelling'. In chapter 9, I finally reject the claim that there is nothing we can do to promote the turn to a new condition of our culture. Though they may be modest, there are steps we can take in order to 'foster the saving power in its increase', and which we will take if we become 'dwellers'. Among the several meanings contained in the rich and complex remark that 'only a God can save us', the idea that we are the impotent spectators of history is not to be found.

1   Being, truth and metaphysics

1. Heidegger's philosophy has a great deal to say about the first and last things that confront each of us as we attempt to live our lives as best we may. His discussions of, *inter alia*, art, death, alienation, technology, community and ecology are, as the Germans say *actuell*, of evident 'relevance' to our existential concerns, the kinds of discussions non-philosophers look to philosophers to provide (but are, these days, often disappointed). For all of this manifest 'relevance', however, the centre of Heidegger's philosophy lies in none of the above topics but in, rather, his *Seinsphilosophie*, his 'philosophy of Being'. The concern with Being – *the* 'matter of thinking', for Heidegger – is so fundamental to all of his work, both early and late, that unless one attains a solid comprehension of what he has to say about it one's grasp of his discussions of the other, initially more accessible, topics is bound to remain superficial and insecure. So it is that in this first chapter we need to begin with the seemingly dry constellation of topics itemized in its somewhat forbidding title. (*Seemingly* but not really dry: the excitement of Heidegger's philosophy is the discovery that the first and last things in the philosophy of Being, properly understood, are also the first and last things in life.)

Truth

2. First and foremost, then, the '*Seinsfrage*', the 'question of Being': what is it? One of Heidegger's statements about Being is that it constitutes 'the hidden essence [*Wesen*] of truth' (DT p. 83), a linking of topics which suggests that truth might be a fruitful point of entry into the topic of Being.

What, then, is truth? Unlike the impatient Pilate, Heidegger devoted a lifetime to providing, in full, an answer to this question. The first major formulation of his account of truth occurred in 1925, in *Plato's Sophist*[1], and

---

[1] Trans. R. Rojcewicz (Bloomington: Indiana University Press, 1997).

received a major restatement in section 44 of *Being and Time* (1927). Its implications were not, however, properly understood in that work which is the reason why later Heidegger views his early masterpiece as, for all its insights, fundamentally flawed.[2] A useful 'take', indeed, on his life's work, it seems to me, is to describe it as the endeavour fully to understand and appropriate all of the ramifications of *Being and Time*'s theory of truth. An improved restatement of the theory occurs in the 1930 'On the Essence of Truth' (ET) an essay he identifies as the beginning of the 'turn' (away from 'metaphysics') that separates later from early Heidegger (LH p. 250). A further restatement occurs in 1936 in 'The Origin of the Work of Art' (OWA pp. 50ff.) and thereafter in many later works.

What then, to repeat, is truth? According to the Western philosophical tradition it is 'correspondence' or, as Heidegger, following the Medievals, calls it, 'adequacy'. Truth is a property of 'propositions' or 'statements', a property they possess when they correspond – are 'adequate to' – the facts. What, however, asks Heidegger, tells us what the facts are to which propositions are to be compared for correspondence (OWA p. 51)?

One answer – the answer, he suggests, provided by the Western tradition in general – is that you just look and see. So, for example, if someone says 'Betty is very thin' you look at what 'Betty' stands for – if there is any doubt about what that is the speaker will simply point – and see whether it is thin or not.

Let us, then, try to apply this simple procedure. I say, pointing, 'Betty is very thin.' You, seeing that what I am pointing at is a rather portly little horse, decide I have said something false. In fact, however, that to which I intended

---

[2] In *Being and Time*, he says, 'metaphysics . . . is still dominant' (LH p. 256). Since, as we will shortly see, later Heidegger takes his central task to be the overcoming of 'metaphysics', this judgment is the basis of his description of *Being and Time* as constituting (along with all his work from 1927 to 1936) a 'false turning [*Holzweg*] albeit a necessary [i.e. productive] one' (GA 15 p. 366).

'*Holzweg*' I take to be intended to describe the *dominant* character of the period and to be, therefore, consistent with particular works – conspicuously the 1930 'On the Essence of Truth' which (as the main text is about to remark) Heidegger describes as the beginning of the 'turn' to his later thinking – being genuinely free of 'metaphysics'. One may perhaps think of 1927–36 as analogous to late winter with isolated works, the 'Essence of Truth' and parts of 'The Origin of the Work of Art', in particular, representing the first buds of spring. This mixed or transitional character of the period is the reason scholars interested in a finer-grained periodization of Heidegger's career than I, at present, am, have identified it as a 'middle' period. On the periodization of Heidegger's 'path of thinking' see, further, HPA p. 3.

to refer was (for my own arcane reasons) not the horse but rather its skin, a skin which is indeed very thin. Or, to change the example, perhaps I say, pointing at the horse, 'That's very old.' You, knowing the horse to be but a foal, decide that I have said something false. In fact, however, that to which I intended to refer (for, again, my own arcane reasons) was not the horse but rather the region of space it exactly occupies.

These examples are, of course, extraordinarily far-fetched. They are, none-theless, revealing, for they show that the mere correlation of words with bits of reality – merely saying '"Betty" stands for *that*' and pointing – is insufficient to determine reference. Normally, of course, communication flows smoothly and we do not suffer from the kinds of misunderstandings illustrated by these examples. Communication is usually unproblematic. But that is only because we share a – usually unnoticed – background understanding as to the kinds of entities that are being talked about. Generally, for example, we share the assumption that the things named and pointed to are whole natural objects rather than their surfaces or the spaces they occupy. What the far-fetched examples reveal, however, is that it is only because of such a background assumption that we know what kinds of things, and hence what kinds of facts, are under discussion. Heidegger calls such a background understanding a 'horizon' (DT p. 63), a horizon of 'disclosure' ('revealing', 'unconcealment'). Sometimes, echoing Nietzsche, he calls it a 'perspective' (QB *passim*).

Heidegger does not deny that truth is correspondence. His point is rather that since the possibility of propositions being true or false (the possibility, as I shall put it, of reality's becoming 'intelligible' to us) depends on there being things to which they refer and facts about those things to which they may or may not correspond, and since the identification of such a realm of facts depends on a horizon of disclosure which alone makes it possible, truth as correspondence is dependent on a something more 'primordial'. This con-dition of the possibility of propositional truth Heidegger calls 'truth as dis-closure' or often, using the Greek word, '*aletheia*' (OWA p. 51) – *a-letheia*, bringing out of 'oblivion' or concealment.

Truth as disclosure, says Heidegger, is always simultaneously 'concealment' (ET p. 148, OWA pp. 53–4). This is how it makes truth as correspondence possible. The horizon of whole natural objects puts out of consideration, blocks, conceals, 'denies' (OWA p. 54) both the horizon of surfaces and that of spaces. But this means that horizons of disclosure also block access to certain truths. If our talk is confined to whole natural objects then truths about their surfaces or spaces are not allowed to appear. This is why Heidegger says that 'truth is un-truth' (not to be confused with falsehood) since there always 'belongs to it the reservoir[3] of the not-yet-uncovered, the uncovered in the sense of concealment' (OWA p. 60).

Heidegger calls that which truth conceals (from now on when I use 'truth' without qualification I mean truth as disclosure) 'the mystery' (ET p. 148). Because of the hidden 'reservoir', the hidden 'depth' (compare BT 152) to truth, truth is 'uncanny' (OWA p. 54), 'awesome' (OWA p. 68). Initially, this is a puzzling inference. Though the whole natural object horizon may block, for now, the spaces and surfaces horizons, the blockage is merely temporary. We can, if we want, choose at a later date to inhabit those other horizons, to discuss reality from a spaces or surfaces 'perspective'.

Heidegger, however, when he speaks of horizons of disclosure means *ultimate* horizons. The horizons discussed so far are, as one might put it, optional. I may adopt and abandon them as, more or less, the mood takes me. My Heideggerian horizon, however, is non-optional. It is, he says, 'transcendental' (DT p. 63), that is (to stay with Kant's language), an '*a priori*' feature of my existence, something which, as a member of the current epoch of the historical culture to which I belong, I inhabit as a matter of necessity. Embodied in the language I speak – language understood broadly as social practice (HE p. 301) or, as Wittgenstein puts it, 'form of life' – it constitutes for me and my fellows, the limit of what, to us, is intelligible. It is, as it were, the horizon of all our horizons. In 'The Origin of the Work of Art', Heidegger calls it a 'world' – 'world' in the 'ontological' sense which is not to be confused with 'world' in the 'ontic' sense of the totality of beings that are disclosed by world in the first sense (AWP p. 129, DT p. 76). In *Being and Time* he calls it the 'thrownness' in which one finds oneself 'already' as one becomes an adult human being and which constitutes one as the kind of human being one is. Language, as Heidegger puts it in the *Introduction to Metaphysics*, is not something man has as an attribute. Rather, language is 'the happening that has man', the 'process through

---

[3] *Herkunftsbereich*. Literally, 'originating region'.

which man first enters history as a being (IM p. 141; compare GA 39 section 7 (h)).[4]

To suppose the limits of intelligibility for my historical-cultural epoch to be also the limits of intelligibility *per se* would be the height of irrational epistemological chauvinism. Once one understands the notion of a transcendental horizon and sees its historically and culturally relative character,[5] the conclusion presents itself that in addition to what is intelligible to us, reality possesses an indefinitely large number of aspects, a 'plenitude' (*Vollzähligkeit*) of 'sides' or 'facets' (*Seiten*) (WPF p. 124, DT p. 64) which would be disclosed to us were we to inhabit transcendental horizons other than the one we do, horizons which, however, we can neither inhabit nor even conceive. Truth, then, is concealment, ultimate truth concealment of the, to us, *ineluctably* mysterious. In 'The Origin of the Work of Art' Heidegger calls this 'region' (see footnote 3 above) 'earth' (*Erde*). 'World' (in the ontic sense) is the intelligible in truth, that which is 'lit up'; as Heidegger calls it, 'the clearing' (*Lichtung*).[6] 'Earth', on the other hand, is 'the not ['linguistically'] mastered [the]... concealed, the disconcerting [*Beirrendes*]' (OWA p. 55), the dark penumbra of unintelligibility that surrounds (and in an important sense, as we will see in later chapters, grounds) our human existence.

---

[4] Kant views the horizon of human world-disclosure – 'the categories' – (though he would not, of course, put it this way) as a kind of 'software programme' that is 'hardwired' into the human being as such, hardwired at all times and places. For Heidegger, however, world-disclosure is embodied in the much more malleable phenomenon of 'language', language considered as social practice. This yields a more fluid picture of horizons of intelligibility than is allowed by Kant, a fact which might lead one to question the appropriateness of Heidegger's describing one's ultimate horizon as 'transcendental'. I think that Heidegger would reply that though world-disclosure is indeed a malleable phenomenon, to the extent that it changes so does the human being. A radical transformation in my ultimate horizon of disclosure (I emigrate to Japan and acquire a native competence in Japanese while gradually losing my competence in English) makes me a new person. Hence the world-disclosure into which I am 'thrown' remains 'transcendental' for me and my 'generation' (BT 385), a necessary and defining feature of *our* existence.

[5] Notice that while horizons of disclosure are dependent on social practices and are hence relative to particular cultures, it does not follow that truth (as correspondence) is. That the *medium* of discovery is (for short) 'subjective' does not entail that *what* is discovered is dependent on us. And the latter proposition Heidegger denies. Though Newton's Laws were not true (or false) before Newton formulated them (BT 226–7), 'for nature [reality, Being] to be as it is does not need... unveiledness' (BP p. 220). Newton discovered (at least approximately) a human-being independent feature of reality itself.

[6] Notice that world in the ontological sense is not the clearing. It is rather that which 'clears' (creates) the clearing. More accurately, 'the clearing' can only refer to world in the ontological sense if 'clearing' is understood as a *verbal* noun, as referring to the activity which, as it were, releases the totality of beings in the midst of which we find ourselves.

Notice that in contrast to the simplicity of the correspondence theory, truth, on Heidegger's account, is *complex*. It is a complex of four elements; the undisclosed (earth), the disclosed (world in the ontic sense), the horizon of disclosure (world in the ontological sense), and man, the discloser. Heidegger records this complexity by calling truth a 'constellation'. To achieve 'insight into that which is' (TT p. 47) (and everything which we will discover that to entail) we must, he says, 'look into the constellation of truth' (QCT p. 33).

being

3. So much for 'truth'. What now of 'Being'? What, to repeat, is Being?

Readers possessing even a slight acquaintance with the secondary literature on Heidegger will have noticed its indecision as to whether 'Being' is to be written with a large or a small 'b'. (The secondary literature in English; in German, since all nouns are capitalized, and since Heidegger almost always uses *Sein* as a noun, the issue does not arise.) This indecision, I shall suggest, is due to the fact that, without being very helpful or consistently explicit about it, Heidegger in fact uses the term in *two* central senses. (One senses that at times he himself struggled to be totally clear on the matter.) Readers who capitalize respond to one, those who do not, respond to the other of these senses. It is, however, I shall argue, important to respond to both. The one sense I shall mark with the small 'b' the other with the large. (The acute reader, noting that I have capitalized up to now, might reasonably conclude that the capitalized sense is, in my view, the most important, that my fundamental sympathies lie with the capitalizers.) When I wish to remain neutral as to which sense is intended, or when I think that both are, I shall either retreat to the German *Sein* or else write 'B/being'.

In the small 'b' sense, being is, as Heidegger puts it, 'presence' (TB p. 2, ID p. 18, WCT p. 235), or sometimes 'presencing' (QB p. 308). Presence (*Anwesenheit*) is contrasted with 'what presences [*das Anwesende*]' (QB p. 299, D p. 163). Since the essence of a being [*das Seiende*] is that it is something present, noticeable, capable of being of 'concern' (TB p. 23) to us, 'what presences' is just another name for beings. While beings are 'ontic', being, i.e. presence, as, not a being but rather, in a yet-to-be-explored sense, the underlying 'ground' of beings (QB p. 300), is 'ontological' (DT p. 76).[7]

Reflecting on the affinities between his own conception of being and Ernst Jünger's (Hegel-indebted) conception of the world-historical, epoch-determining *Gestalt* (for Jünger, as we will see, the *Gestalt* that defines modernity is that of 'the worker'), Heidegger says that like Jünger's *Gestalt*, being is 'transcendence', that is, 'the meta-physical' (QB pp. 298–9). It transcends beings, is 'above' the 'physical', in the way in which the visual field transcends 'the appearance of objects' (DT p. 63).

Thinking about the 'presence' – 'what presences' relation in terms of this optical analogy suggests there to be two aspects to the relation between being and beings. First, as the visual field is necessary to there being any objects of sight at all, so, one may assume, presence is necessary to there being anything at all that presences. Only being renders it possible that beings should show up for us at all. Second, as, in Jünger's language, the 'optics' (QB p. 294) of a visual field determine the character of its contents – to someone who has lost the sense of colour only the tonal contrasts between things can show up – so presence limits our 'representing' (DT p. 64) of beings, the way in which they can show up for us. Heidegger sums up both these aspects of being's 'transcendence' of beings in the following passage. Presence, he says, is

that which, as ground, already underlies everything present as that presence . . . and thus 'legitimizes' the latter *as* beings, . . . in the sense of [being their] authoritative, underlying ground. (QB p. 300)

Presence, says Heidegger, 'the *transcendens* pure and simple (*Being and Time* section 7)', is that which 'prevails . . . in an authoritative manner' (QB p. 312).

It is obvious from the preceding remarks that 'being' in the small 'b' sense is just a synonym for that which, in discussing truth, Heidegger refers to as a (fundamental) horizon of disclosure and as 'world' in the ontological sense. The three phrases are alternative descriptions of that which, both when talking about B/being and when talking about truth, he calls 'the transcendental': that which transcends beings and, in the two ways just discussed, determines the

---

[7] In *Being and Time* Heidegger explains that an 'ontic' investigation is an investigation of some range of beings – biology, for example, investigates living beings – while an 'ontological' investigation investigates the conditions of there being beings as such. The Kantian investigation that discovers the 'categories of the understanding' is an example of the latter.

way in which they show up for ('presence' to) us. In this sense, then, being (more accurately, a particular understanding, 'clearing',[8] or, in the language of *Being and Time*, 'meaning' of B/being) is that fundamental disclosure which is embodied in the 'linguistic' practices of a given culture in a given epoch of its historical existence. It is for this reason that Heidegger says that being exists only through human (by which he means language-using[9]) being. 'Only man', he says,

open for being, allows this to arrive as presence. Presence needs the open of a clearing[10] and remains as such through this dependence given over [*übereignet*] to human being. (ID p. 19)

This, however, he adds does not mean human beings are *prior* to being since though being is dependent on man, man is equally dependent on the clearing of being (*ibid.*). In, for example, the world defined by Jünger's *Gestalt* of the worker, the world where everything shows up as either ripe for work or the product of work, the human being shows up as, and only as, 'the worker'. In other clearings he shows up in other ways. Man's nature is his clearing. 'I am', as Wittgenstein observed, 'my world'. (Lower case) being and human being are, therefore, to put the point in Heideggerian language, 'equiprimordial'.

Being

4. So much for being. For many readers, so much, too, for *Sein* as such. For them – for indeed, most of the time at least, the author of *Being and Time* – all there is to say about *Sein* is that it is 'intelligibility' (BT 152).[11]

I oppose this view of things. Though there is indeed *a* sense of *Sein* in which it is just presence (truth as disclosure, 'world' in the ontological sense, intelligibility), there is another sense in which what is crucial about it is precisely the opposite – *un*intelligibility ('un-truth'). In the language of 'The Origin of

---

[8] The participle, here, needs to be understood verbally rather than substantively, as referrring to that which *produces*, 'clears', the clearing in the sense of the ontic world. See footnote 6 above.
[9] All his life Heidegger opposed biological conceptions of the human essence (see HPN chapter 1 section 16). For him, the human essence is to be a 'language' user, a world discloser. It follows that beings biologically quite other than ourselves would count, for Heidegger, as instances of 'man' provided only that they were 'language' users, bearers of a culture.
[10] Again, the participle is to be understood verbally rather than substantively. See footnote 8 above.
[11] This is the reason that later Heidegger views the work as, for all its insights, fundamentally flawed, a 'dead end [*Holzweg*]' (GA 15 p. 366) irredeemably dominated by 'oblivion of Being', by the 'metaphysics' which it is later Heidegger's prime task to overcome (see footnote 2 above).

the Work of Art', while in one sense *Sein* is just 'world' (in the ontological sense), in a different and, in the end, much more important sense its heart lies in 'earth'. More accurately, *Sein* in this second sense is 'world' (in the ontic sense) and 'earth' taken together, in other words, 'that which really is' (TT p. 44) or simply 'reality' (QCT p. 18)[12] taken in the infinite 'plenitude' of all its 'facets'. It is this second sense I indicate by writing 'Being' with a capital 'B'.

5. Why should we acknowledge Being in addition to being? Why, in other words, should we acknowledge that key Heideggerian phrases – 'house of B/being', 'destiny of B/being', 'truth of B/being', 'O/other of beings', for example – are systematically ambiguous?[13] For a number of reasons, the first of which has to do with Heidegger's terminology.

Though by no means consistently, Heidegger sometimes observes a distinction between '*Sein*' and '*Seyn*' (see, for example, GA 39 *passim* and ET p. 144 footnote a). The use of the antique 'y' suggests something both solemn and forgotten. The (generally excellent) translator of 'On the Essence of Truth' renders the '*Sein*'-'*Seyn*' distinction in English as a distinction between 'being' and 'beyng' (*ibid.*). Though ingenious, this strikes me as an unilluminating rendition. I prefer to use the 'being'-'Being' distinction. Given that the 'y' is intended to suggest something solemn and forgotten, its similarity to the 'god'-'God' distinction is a useful one.

---

[12] Of course 'world' is often used, and is used by Heidegger, as a synonym for 'reality', 'as a name for that which is, in its entirety' (AWP p. 129). ('The world', Wittgenstein famously said – though not with Heidegger's sense of totality – 'is all that is the case'.) This marks a third sense, distinct from both the 'ontological' and 'ontic' senses, in which the term will figure in this book.

[13] A most infuriating ambiguity which permeates Heidegger's later writings is that between the subjective (or 'active') and objective (or 'passive') genitive. ('Tales of Hoffmann' read as 'tales *told by* Hoffmann' is a subjective genitive while read as 'tales *about* Hoffmann' it is an objective genitive.) Depending on which is intended 'house of B/being' (as in the refrain 'language is the house of B/being' (WPF p. 132 *et passim*)) means either 'house "built" by Being' or 'house inhabited by being' and 'truth of B/being' means either 'truth "sent" by Being' or 'truth which is being'. (Notice that Being determines a subjective, being an objective genitive.) Sometimes, but by no means consistently, as the main text is about to remark, Heidegger does distinguish the senses by writing '*Sein*' in the normal way when he means 'being' and '*Seyn*' with the antique 'y' when he means 'Being'. The reason, however, he does not observe this disambiguating convention at all consistently is that, nearly all of the time, the ambiguous utterances express what he takes to be important truths on *both* readings. 'Language is the house of B/being', for example, he takes to be true both in the sense that the 'house' is 'built' ('sent') by Being and in the sense that it is 'inhabited' by being, is where being is to be found. The economy and poetic richness of expression that results from this willful ambiguity, however, in no way makes up for the disastrous loss of clarity that results.

Again, sometimes but by no means consistently, Heidegger observes a distinction between 'Being' *simpliciter* or 'Being as Being' and 'the being [or 'beingness'] of beings' which is treated as synonymous with 'the truth of beings' (see, for example, IWM p. 280, LH p. 246, OWA p. 39 and N III pp. 150–8). 'Being as Being' I take to be Being, 'the being of beings' to be being.

6. The second reason for acknowledging Being in addition to being is that there are a number of passages in which, a little reluctantly, perhaps,[14] Heidegger comes clean and, reasonably explicitly, *says* that *Sein* has two senses.

In 'What are Poets for?', for example, while emphasizing that it should not be taken too literally, Heidegger adopts as his own Rilke's image of Being as a sphere which, like the moon, has a lighted side ('world') and a dark side ('earth'). Referring to this 'globe of Being' he says that we may distinguish two senses of *Sein*: 'being in the sense of lightening-unifying presence' and Being in the sense of 'beings in . . . the plenitude of all their facets' (WPF p. 124). A similar passage occurs in the 'Conversation on a Country Path'. Since our world-disclosure is 'but the side facing us of an openness which surrounds us; an openness which is filled with views[15] of the appearances of what are to our re-presenting objects'[16] we need, says Heidegger, a special term to designate this 'openness' (DT pp. 64–5). In the 'Conversation' the term chosen is not 'Being', but rather the mysterious 'that which regions'. But it is clear that this must mean 'Being' rather than 'being' since its referent 'can be thought of neither as ontic [a being or totality of beings] nor as ontological

---

[14] Heidegger, it is clear, sometimes deliberately cultivates an air, not merely of mystery, but of mystification. Take, for example, the remarks about the genitive in the previous footnote. Heidegger *knows* perfectly well that his use of the genitive is obscure – in 'Anaximander's Saying' he refers to 'the enigmatically ambiguous genitive' (GA 5 p. 364) – yet never seeks to clarify it. In an imperfect world, it is not uncommon to find genius go hand in hand with a touch of charlatanry (or, more charitably, showmanship).

[15] Notice that 'views' do not entail a viewer: there are undoubtedly many fine views in Antarctica which no one has yet seen. Heidegger's talk of alternative views, or aspects, of things by no means commits him to alternative viewers.

[16] Notice (though Heidegger is not always clear about this) that the predicate 'is a being' is always relative to a particular horizon of disclosure. What is individuated as a being in one disclosure may not be so individuated in another. The individual of one disclosure may appear as a mere part of an individual, or as a congregation of individuals, in another. It follows that that of which there are many 'views', that, in other words which is, in Heideggerian language, persistently 'the same' through many disclosures, is not a being. There is no familiar word to describe this persistent sameness. One might, perhaps, call it a 'ripple' in the real.

[the horizon of presence which determines the way in which beings show up for us]' (DT p. 76).

A second passage occurs in the interview with Richard Wisser broadcast on ZDF television in 1969. To Wisser's observation that the 'question of *Sein* [*Seinsfrage*]' is the 'basic question' of his philosophy Heidegger responds that 'the phrase "question of B/being" is ambiguous'. On the one hand it requests a 'definition' of *Sein*, but on the other 'it can be understood in the following sense: whereon is each answer to the [above] question of being based i.e. wherein, after all is the unconcealment of being grounded?'[17] This passage only makes sense if we take the '*Sein*', here, to be being and that in which it is 'grounded' to be Being.

This distinction between ground and grounded occurs, too, in the distinction between 'being' and 'the essence of being' that runs through 'On the Question of Being'. The 'essence of being' may, Heidegger suggests, be called '*Sein*' (QB p. 309), a suggestion which makes no sense unless we distinguish between the two senses of 'B/being' and take this *Sein* to be Being.

In a 1954 footnote to the 1930 'On The Essence of Truth' Heidegger distinguishes three senses of 'essence': '(1) *quidditas* – the "what" – khoinon (2) enabling – condition of possibility; (3) ground of enabling' (ET p. 136 footnote a). In which of these senses could Being be the essence of being? Not, obviously, in the first sense – only beings have a 'whatness' (that which is given by the definition of what it is to be a being of a certain kind). And not in the second sense either. (Lower case) being, clearly, is the 'condition of the possibility' of our apprehension of beings, as the visual field is the 'condition of the possibility' of our apprehension of visual objects, and the idea of a condition of the possibility of a condition of possibility is baroque to the point of senselessness. The relevant sense, therefore, is clearly the third: being is the condition of the possibility of our apprehension of beings and Being is the 'ground' of being, that in virtue of which a given mode or meaning of being obtains, 'that in which *aletheia* is grounded' (QB p. 314). This is the reason Heidegger refers to Being so often as 'the Origin' or 'Source' (see DK p. 214, I pp. 129ff., WCT pp. 350–1, TB p. 12 and footnote 3 above). In some way (a way that has often been thought to be problematic – see footnote 24 below) Heidegger thinks of Being as the *generative* 'ground' of being.

---

[17] *Martin Heidegger in Conversation* ed. R. Wisser, trans. B. Murthy (New Delhi: Arnold-Heinemann, 1977) pp. 44–5, hereafter HIC.

It seems, then, that we can say this: that while being is the *transcendental* ground of our world of beings, Being, as the generative ground of being, is its *generative* ground.

A final important passage is that in which Heidegger performs the celebrated act of writing *Sein* with a crossing-out through it: ~~Sein~~. This crossing-out has, he says, two functions. The first is an 'initial' and merely 'preventative' one of blocking 'the almost ineradicable habit or representing 'being' as something standing somewhere on its own' in complete 'independence' of 'human being' (QB p. 310). (I shall discuss this passage in detail in section 14 below.) Because the existence of beings[18] is entirely independent of human being, and because there is a powerful tendency built into every Western language to assume a substance wherever there is a substantive, a being wherever there is a noun (ID p. 66), we are powerfully tempted to assume that 'being' designated something that is entirely independent of human being. Hence some radically disruptive device is needed to warn and remind us that 'being' does not function at all like a common or garden noun, that 'being' is not a being, that it is 'nothing' (QB p. 317) (no thing), no more a being than the visual field is an object of sight.[19] The point, then, in other language, is to mark the 'ontological difference' between being and beings (ID pp. 33ff.), to mark the fact that the status of being is 'ontological' rather than 'ontic'. (The question of why it is of such importance to be alive to the ontological difference will be discussed in section 11 below.)

The main point of the crossing-out, however, says Heidegger, is not the 'merely negative' one just outlined. Its primary significance is that the four arms of the crossing 'point . . . toward the four regions of the fourfold and their being gathered in the locale of this crossing through' (QB pp. 310–11).

What 'the fourfold' is will be discussed in detail in chapter 7. Let me here, however, briefly anticipate that discussion. Later Heidegger holds that the fundamental structure of the (ontic) world – any world of human habitation – has four, as it were, dimensions to it, dimensions which he calls 'earth', 'sky', 'gods' and 'mortals'. It only shows up as 'the fourfold', however, in that

---

[18] More accurately, of those 'ripples' in the real which are individuated in our disclosure as beings. See footnote 16 above.

[19] There is an interesting anticipation of this point in *Being and Time*'s discussion of 'the One' (*das Man*). In expounding the concept Heidegger points out that 'traditional logic' ranging ('quantifying', as logicians say) over beings alone, 'fails' with respect to the One, cannot acknowledge it (BT 128–9).

moment of 'insight' or 'in-flashing' (TT p. 45) in which it shows up as a 'holy' or sublime place: in which, according to Heidegger's analysis of the sublime, it is intuitively grasped as the lighted side of the 'globe of Being', a globe the other side of which is the 'unfathomable' (WPF p. 128) 'mystery'.

If this is right, then the two functions of the crossing-out point to the two senses of '*Sein*'. On the one hand it points to being in its ontological difference from beings. On the other hand it points to the fourfold, to the manifest grasped in conjunction with the hidden side of reality, in short, to Being.

7. One reason, then, for acknowledging Being in addition to being is that on various occasions and in various ways, Heidegger reasonably clearly acknowledges such a distinction himself. Another lies in the fact that he says, as already noted, that '*Sein* is what really is' (TT p. 44), in other words 'the real' (QCT p. 23), reality. Since, however, being is, as we have seen, human-being-dependent, the supposition that 'being' exhausts the meaning of '*Sein*' leads to the absurdly idealist conclusion that nothing 'real' antedated the existence of man. To avoid this conclusion, as Heidegger clearly wishes to do (see footnote 5 above), we must distinguish Being from being and take the former to be 'that which is in its entirety' (AWP p. 129); that is to say, reality as it presents itself to ('presences' for) us, together with all those other 'views' of it which lie beyond the horizon of our intelligibility.

8. A further reason – the most crucial of all – for the acknowledgment of Being consists in the distortion of Heideggerian thinking – oblivion, in my view, to its heart and ultimate concern – which results from the failure to do so.

Being is, says Heidegger, *the* 'matter of thinking' that which, above all, is '*fragewürdig* [thought-provoking or question-worthy]'. Though it 'withdraws' from us it also

draws us along by its very withdrawal, whether we become aware of it immediately, or at all. Once we are drawn into the withdrawal, we are, somewhat like migratory birds, but in an entirely different way, caught in the pull of what draws, attracts us by its withdrawal. And once we, being so attracted, are drawing toward what draws us, our essential being already bears the stamp of that 'pull'. As we are drawing toward what withdraws, we ourselves point toward it. (BW pp. 350–1)

It is in such pointing, that 'man first is man' (*ibid.*). If we reach out to what draws and withdraws we are drawn into the 'enigmatic nearness of its appeal'.

As one who placed his whole life in this 'draft', Socrates is the 'purest thinker of the West'. All thinkers after him, even the greatest, have been 'fugitives from the draft' (BW p. 358).

Not, however, the poets. Summarizing the experience of Being recorded in Rilke's poetry, Heidegger explains that, for the poet, we are the beings who are 'ventured forth' into existence by the '*Urgrund*', yet at the same time held in the 'gravitational pull' of a 'draft [*Bezug* – 'pull' not 'push']' which, whether we admit it or not, draws us back to itself as the self-withdrawing 'centre' (WPF pp. 99–107). The 'destitution' of modernity, according to Heidegger's reading of Rilke, is its oblivion to 'the drawing of the pure draft' (WPF p. 108), the fact that contemporary man 'completely blocks' his path into the draft (WPF p. 116).

As he intimates in his appropriation of Rilke, the need of modernity, according to Heidegger, is the recovery of our nearness to 'the Open', as Rilke calls his '*Urgrund*'. This, above all, is the matter of thinking (which is not at all to say that it is the exclusive preserve of professional thinkers). The salvation of modernity requires we once more attend to that which, above all, is 'worthy' of thought.

9. What kind of thinking (to digress, for a little while, from the main line of discussion) is required to think the *Urgrund*? Heidegger distinguishes two kinds of redemptive thinking: *Dichten* (poetry) and *Denken* (thinking) (S p. 106). It is important to notice here that, contrary to appearances, this is not a contrast *between* poetry and thought since, for Heidegger, 'valid' (WPF p. 96) poetry is always *also* thinking, is always 'thinking poetry' (WPF p. 95). (Heidegger's highest exemplars of such poetry are Sophocles and Hölderlin.) The contrast is rather, therefore, a contrast between different *kinds* of thinking. *Denken* is what Heidegger also calls 'meditative thinking'. It is his own philosophical thinking about, centrally, the essence of truth. Meditative thinking is philosophical thinking which, properly carried out, leads to one's 'openness to the mystery' (DT p. 55). *Dichten*, on the other hand, is what Heidegger calls 'poetic thinking' or, appropriating the title of the Hölderlin poem which concerned him more than any other, 'recollective thinking [*Andenken*]' (QB p. 314). Thinking of this kind is contrasted with 'representational thinking'. Whereas the latter always occurs *within* a horizon of disclosure, the former is, in a certain sense, 'horizonless'. Thinking of this kind 'has the task of attending to [the] ... concealment in which

unconcealment (*aletheia*) is grounded' (*ibid.*), the task of 'founding the holy' (GA 52 p. 193, I p. 138, GA 4 p. 148). It is thinking which brings 'the mystery' to presence while allowing it to remain the mystery (QB p. 320), allowing it to remain 'nameless' (LH p. 243).[20]

Both meditative and poetic thinking, then, allow 'the holy enigma [*Rätsel*]' to come 'close' to us 'as the enigma' (I pp. 34–5), allow us to 'grasp the ungraspable' and our lives as lived 'in the face of the ungraspable' (I p. 136). '[W]hen poesy is elevated and thinking profound' they think 'the same' (WCT p. 20). It follows that, *contra* Plato, they are, at the most fundamental level, friends and allies. As Heidegger puts it in his poem 'Cézanne' (whom he regards as a 'poet' *par excellence*) they 'belong together' (D p. 163; see, too, I p. 111).

Why, then, does there remain between them an essential difference, one which, Heidegger insists, must never be obscured (I p. 112)? Why is it that though what they say is 'the same', it is 'never identical' (WCT p. 20)? Why, though they both think and say 'the holy', is there a 'clean and decisive cleft' (*ibid.*) between the *ways* in which they do so?

Heidegger recognizes, I think, five essential differences between meditative and poetic thinking. The first is that the former is discursive, is a process of reasoning – 'brainracking' as he at one point puts it (HIC p. 46) – while the latter is intuitive, 'direct'. 'These days in Cézanne's homeland', Heidegger is recorded to have said on one of his visits to Provence in the 1960s, 'are worth more than a whole library of philosophy books. If only one could think as directly as Cézanne painted' (quoted in HPA p. 151; see chapter 4 sections 19–20 of that work for a detailed discussion of Heidegger's relationship to Cézanne). The former (to borrow from Schopenhauer a metaphor he uses in an entirely different context) slowly circles the fortress of the mystery from without, the latter, as if by a secret, underground passage, places us directly in it.

The second reason for Heidegger's insistence on the essential difference between the two lies, I would suggest, in the fact that, along with that of all the other sciences, philosophical[21] thinking is a species of 'representational', horizon-bound thinking. This means that while great poetry, in its own way,

---

[20] For a detailed discussion of Heidegger's view of poetry, of what distinguishes it from prose and of why it should have, *qua* poetry, the special task of 'thematizing' the holy, see HPA chapter 3 section 17.

[21] As observed in the Introduction, though Heidegger sometimes represents his 'meditative thinking' as something other than philosophical thinking, in reality, this only means other than *bad* philosophical thinking.

brings the 'holy mystery' to positive presence – 'thematizes' it – meditative thinking can only indicate its presence negatively, by indicating that there is 'something [*etwas*] completely and utterly Other [*Anderes*]' (GA 15 p. 363) than everything that lies within the domain that it is competent to talk about.

Schopenhauer, discussing the relation between mysticism ('illuminism') and philosophy, while insisting that the former can represent genuine knowledge that is of ultimate importance, insists, too, that such knowledge is incapable of literal communication. Philosophy, however,

should be communicable knowledge and must therefore be rationalism. Accordingly, at the end of my philosophy I have indicated the sphere of illuminism as something that exists, but I have guarded against setting even one foot thereon.[22]

This, I think, is Heidegger's position with respect to philosophy. Meditative thinking 'ends' by 'indicating' the sphere of 'the mystery' but remains, itself, outside. Only poetic thinking 'sets foot thereon', brings the mystery to positive presence. This is not, however, to say that the Heideggerian *texts* end where meditative thinking ends. The single most striking difference between early and later texts is that whereas the former remain pure (or nearly pure) philosophy, the latter are a complementary mingling of both meditative and poetic thinking, a happy marriage between the two. (The appearance of the latter, of course, is what leads the staid to dismiss later Heidegger as 'mere poetry' or 'mere mysticism'.) Whereas, that is to say, Wittgenstein's response to the mystical was to demand that one lapse into a Trappist silence – 'Whereof we cannot speak we must remain silent' – Heidegger's response is to become a poet.

The third difference between meditative and poetic thinking I suggest Heidegger to have recognized, is a consequence of the second. Because the latter brings to positive presence what the former can only indicate negatively, it possesses a kind of 'power' (GA 39 p. 214) the former does not. This is one way in which poetic thinking is superior to meditative thinking, why, from, at least, certain points of view, a Cézanne 'is worth a whole library of philosophy books'. So far as power is concerned, a picture is, as we say, worth a thousand words. When it comes to reappropriating 'the mystery' in one's life as well as one's head, the transition from meditative to poetic thinking is essential, since only the latter has the power to engage one's whole being

---

[22] *Parerga and Paralipomena: Short Philosophical Essays*, 2 vols., trans. E. F. J. Payne (Oxford: Clarendon Press, 1974), vol. II p. 10.

and thereby transform one's life. Only in art can the 'decisive confrontation' with the destitution of our age come about (QCT p. 35).

A fourth difference I think Heidegger recognizes between philosophy and poetry is that the latter is, in a certain sense, more (in Heideggerian language), 'primordial'. Schopenhauer says that though philosophy, *qua* philosophy, can never *be* 'illuminism', nonetheless, when it is great philosophy, it rests on, and is guided by, a 'concealed illuminism' (*Parerga and Paralipomena*, vol. II pp. 10–11). This, I think, represents the character of the later (and even, to a degree, the earlier) Heideggerian texts. The ground from which they spring lies, not in any product of ratiocination, but in, rather, poetic vision. *Qua* meditative thinking they attempt, over and over again, with Jamesian obsessiveness, to articulate as much of that vision as can possibly be captured within the limits of the (in Schopenhauer's language) 'rationalism' that is definitive of philosophy. This means that though, as I put it, a 'marriage' between poetry and philosophy occurs in the texts, it is not a marriage between partners who are, in every respect, equals. The generative principle, the principle of fertility, is poetry. This means that, in one respect, the role of philosophy is confined to the traditional one of midwife.

Why, however, it might now be asked, do we need meditative thinking at all? If art is more direct, complete, powerful and fertile than philosophy, why not throw all our philosophy books away, including those by Heidegger, and just make do with art? The answer, it seems to me – and here we come to the fifth difference I take Heidegger to recognize between philosophy and poetry – is that though poetry is prior to philosophy in the *order of generation*, philosophy is prior to poetry in the *order of verification*. What, that is to say, philosophy can do which art cannot is to *validate*. It is the careful 'brainracking' of the Heideggerian meditation on B/being and truth which assures us that the fertile and powerful words of the poets yield insight rather than wishful fancy, truth rather than illusion, that the highest poets ('demigods' (GA 39 *passim*) or 'angels' (WPF pp. 136–7)) are beings we can *trust*. Along with the articulation of vision which it presupposes, this is philosophy's contribution to the happiness of the marriage between it and poetry in the later texts. While poetry 'founds the holy', thinking establishes that there really is a 'holy' to be founded.

10. Heidegger's most common name for the defining affliction ('destitution' (WPF p. 91)) of modernity (to return now from the digression of the previous

section) is 'oblivion (literally 'forgetfulness') of Being [*Seinsvergessenheit*]'. Locked as we are into merely 'calculative thinking' (DT p. 53) (the planning of means to practical ends) Being – reality in the 'plenitude of *all* its "sides" – is what we have become oblivious to. The task of thinking, of both meditative and poetic thinking, is to overcome this oblivion, to raise ourselves to the kind of thinking which, in grasping the ground of our being, 'recollects' Being.

11. The above exposition of Heidegger's thinking towards Being will have been, to those who know no Heidegger, only dimly comprehensible. But only, I think, a dim comprehensibility is necessary to make it clear that Being – 'the Origin', 'the Source', 'the *Ur-etwas* [ur-something]' (GA 6 p. 60), 'the Other [as opposed to 'other'] of beings' (GA 15 p. 363), '*ku*' as it is called in Japanese Zen Buddhism (DL p. 14), '*Tao*' as it is called in Taoism (ID p. 45) – is, first, *the* topic of Heideggerian thinking, and second, as something 'mystical' (QB p. 310), 'awesome' (OWA p. 68), 'holy'(WPF p. 94), is an object of something close to, or identical with, religious venera- tion. This is why those sensitive to the 'theological' heart of Heidegger's think- ing wish to capitalize the 'B' of 'Being' – to exhibit the same kind of veneration towards it as is exhibited by the 'G' of 'God' and the 'y' of Heidegger's '*Seyn*'. Heidegger denies many times that Being is God, but the denials are always made with reference to the god of Christian theology and metaphysics. If however, we think of Being as the god of an authentic (or 'originary') theology – in Greece, says Heidegger, 'theology' was not 'representational thinking' about God but rather 'the mytho-poetic saying of the gods without any relationship to articles of faith or church doctrine' (ID p. 44) – if we think of it as, not the God of Christian dogma, but as, rather, 'the god of the poet',[23] the 'unknown God' who, in Hölderlin's poetry, approaches us in the sight of 'familiar' things (PMD p. 225), then Being, to be brief and blunt, is God. 'Only a God', after all, as the multi-layered title of Heidegger's 1966 interview with *Der Spiegel* puts it, 'can save us' (S p. 91).

Lower case 'being' is incapable of bearing the religious weight of Heidegger's language and concern. By denying Being, by taking the discus- sion of being to be the totality of his *Seinsphilosophie*, one can undoubtedly produce an interesting figure, one very much in tune with the secular tenor of

---

[23] *The Piety of Thinking* trans. J Hart and J. Maraldo (Bloomington: Indiana University Press, 1976) p. 58.

modern Western philosophy. One may even succeed in convincing a few of
the 'flakier' members of the 'analytic' hegemony within modern anglophone
philosophy that Heidegger is, in their own terms, a respectable figure, a genuine philosopher. What one will miss, however, is everything that, to him, is
of ultimate concern. One will bypass the – essentially 'theological' – core
of his 'matter of thinking'. And to the extent that one identifies one's own
thinking with that of this diminished Heidegger one will lapse, oneself, into
Seinsvergessenheit.

12. A final reason for acknowledging Being in addition to being is to be
discovered by attending to the course actually followed by Heidegger's 'path
of thinking' towards Being. This course runs somewhat as follows.

Sein, as Western thinking has always understood it, is, we know, presence.
But what is presence and where, asks Heidegger, does it come from? Presence, we know, is given – something we find ourselves 'already' encircled
by. But what, he asks, does the 'giving' (QB p. 317)? 'Wherein', to repeat
Heidegger's question posed in the Wisser interview, 'is the unconcealment of
being grounded' (see p. 15 above)?

An answer to be rejected is the notion that presence is the product of human
intention. This is evidently false. No 'committee' (QCT p. 23) decides on our
ultimate horizon of disclosure. Though it happens through human language,
disclosure is never human 'handiwork', 'will never let itself be mastered
either positively or negatively by a human doing' (TT p. 38). Human beings
never make their own ultimate horizons of disclosure; conspiracy theories are
always false. This, I think, is a matter not of observation but of logic. Since
conspiring or planning is an instance of what Heidegger calls 'calculative
thinking', and since thinking of this type always presupposes and happens
within a horizon of disclosure, conspiring to create one's ultimate horizon of
disclosure would require one to 'calculate' before one could 'calculate'.

Human beings and human cultures are, therefore, receptive rather than
creative with respect to the modes of presence they inhabit. (The 'languages'
that provide them are, as we say, '*natural* languages'.) Heidegger puts this
by saying modes of presence are 'granted', 'sent' or 'destined' to them. But
what, to repeat, does the 'destining'? Western philosophical thinking has
never asked this question, regarding presence as something 'ultimate and
primordial'. We, however, says Heidegger, need to ponder the 'provenance' of

presence (QB p. 303), to ponder, not just being but, additionally, its 'essence', that is, its originating 'ground' (ET p. 136).

Heidegger calls this 'Source' or 'Origin' the 'It' (his own capitalization); the 'It' that occurs in 'It gives [*Es gibt*] presence'. (The German '*Es gibt*', though generally used to mean 'It is', as in 'It is raining', literally means 'It gives'. What Heidegger intends to suggest is that 'There is presence' is more perspicuously construed as 'It gives presence'.) The 'It', then, 'gives being i.e. presence', 'sends' or 'destines' presence in each of its 'epochal transmutations' (TB p. 17). Yet what is the 'It'?

Perhaps, muses Heidegger, this question has a false presupposition, perhaps it is the product of grammatical illusion. Can it be assumed that anything at all corresponds to the 'It', bearing in mind that neither Latin nor Greek possesses the 'It is . . .' construction? (In Latin, he observes, '*Pluit*' means 'It is raining', in Greek '*chre*' 'It is needful'.) But that, he points out acutely, 'does not mean that which is meant by the "It" is not also in their thought' (TB p. 18).

It would, then, be superficial to dismiss the 'It' as a grammatical chimera. There is an 'It' and this 'It' is Being: 'the "It" that here [in "*Es gibt*"] "gives" is Being itself' (LH pp. 254–5, cf. p. 252). Being, then, 'gives' – 'sends', 'destines' – being.[24] Through the medium of human practice it, as it were,

---

[24] It may be objected that if Being, as well as being the object of disclosure, is its 'Source' then it is, surely, a *cause*. Yet Heidegger insists that anything which preserves the 'mysteriousness of . . . distance' must lie beyond the 'cause-effect coherence' (QCT p. 26). To present Being as a cause is to lapse, it may be claimed, into *Seinsvergessenheit*, into, in Heidegger's pejorative sense of the word that we are about to investigate, 'metaphysics'. More specifically, it is to lapse into that species of metaphysics Heidegger calls 'onto-theology': the metaphysical view which divides reality up into (a) ordinary beings and (b) their cause and creator, a more or less overt 'God' (ID pp. 31ff.). Hence, since the 'Source' and 'Origin' talk is unmistakable in Heidegger his philosophy is fundamentally self-contradictory.

Clearly if Being 'sends' being then it is *responsible for* being and is, in *that* sense (see QCT p. 8), a cause. Actually, however, all that Heidegger insists on is that, as the 'mystery', Being must not be understood as an *efficient* cause, a '*causa efficiens*' (QCT p. 26). What he means, here, by 'efficient' cause is, I suggest, *explanation*. (This is also, I believe, what he means by 'cosmic ground' when he denies (L p. 252) that Being is a cosmic ground.) What deprives Being of its mystery – and is, as such, 'metaphysics' – is the attribution to it (in, for example, mainstream Christian theology) of a *known nature* which is taken to explain the character of the world it discloses. (A close look at what Heidegger means by 'onto-theology' reveals that it is the double movement of the inference from the character of the world to the character of its origin and back again from the character of the origin to the character of the world that in fact defines the position (QB p. 309).) So long as (with Heidegger's heroes, Hölderlin and the Medieval mystic Meister Eckhart) we remember that God or Being is unknown and unknowable – apart from the that and how of its partial self-revelation as world – its mystery is preserved and 'metaphysics' avoided.

kindles a light that makes it visible to itself, allows it to become, in Hegel's language, self-conscious. This giving is a 'self-giving' (LH p. 255), a self-disclosing, but at the same time (since the clearing of what lies within a horizon is always the concealing of what lies beyond) a self-refusal. The 'It' 'gives and refuses itself simultaneously' (*ibid.*). Later Heidegger calls this 'clearing-concealing' (LH p. 249) giving the '*Ereignis*', the '*Ereignis* of presencing' (QB p. 302). The *Ereignis* (which will receive a great deal more discussion later on) is the 'Event' or 'Happening' of Being's self-giving self-refusal.[25]

The 'It', hitherto unthought in (post-Socratic) Western philosophy according to Heidegger (QB p. 249), is, as we have seen, *the* 'matter of thinking'. To ordinary thinking it is totally inaccessible, as inaccessible as the Chinese *Tao* (ID p. 45). Yet, as we have seen, there are other kinds of thinking, above all, Hölderlinian, 'poetic', 'recollective' thinking, which can bring us into the nearness (*die Nähe*) of Being – a Being which remains, nonetheless, as the conceptually ungraspable, utterly distant, 'the furthest' (LH p. 252). Openness to this 'It' which is, in Wim Wenders' phrase, 'Far away' yet, since it discloses *itself* as world, 'so close', is, Heidegger claims, for reasons that we will come to, something we need more than anything else.

In sum, then, to understand Heidegger and follow him along his 'path of thinking' into 'the nearness' we have to think both being and Being and the difference between them. Thinking about the former, if properly carried out, is a stepping-stone to the latter. Thinking about the day, thinking about the clearing, about illumination and the illuminated, leads us into the depths of 'holy night' (WPF p. 94).

Metaphysics

13. Why, however, is it that 'all Western thinking' since Plato has failed to carry out this proper thinking, has failed to follow the path which, once discovered, leads from beings to being and from being to Being, returns us into

---

[25] '*Ereignis*' means a great deal more to Heidegger than 'event'. As a synonym, he suggests 'event of appropriation' (TB p. 19). In translation, however, this substitution makes impenetrable nonsense of many passages (see, for example, T pp. 179–80), for which reason I shall, throughout this study, leave the term untranslated. Why the *Ereignis* should be an 'appropriating' will be discussed later on.

a 'primal relation to Being' (QB p. 281)? Why has the 'It' eluded the West? Heidegger's answer is contained in a single, but difficult word: 'metaphysics'. What, we must therefore ask, (in Heidegger's by no means standard use of the term) is 'metaphysics'?

The subject-matter of metaphysics is, he says, 'the metaphysical'. What this is – the 'meta-physical' – we already know. Properly understood, our cultural-epochal 'metaphysics' is that mode of disclosure/presence/being which over-arches, 'transcends', the beings of our world in the way in which the visual field transcends that which shows up within it. Heidegger emphasizes that in this, non-pejorative, sense, 'metaphysics' has nothing to do with any 'doctrine [or] . . . discipline of philosophy' (QB p. 312).

Philosophical metaphysics, as concerned with the transcendent in the above sense, is concerned with the 'being of beings' (*ibid.*). It is concerned to 'state . . . what beings are as beings' and, as such, its essence is 'ontology' (the science of entities or beings as such) (IWM p. 287). Its concern is to discover the 'beingness of beings', the 'universal traits' (*ibid.*) which all beings, as beings, have.

Nothing, evidently, is wrong with this enterprise as such. Yet as a condition of our culture, Heidegger claims, metaphysics is the 'essence' of contemporary 'nihilism' (QB p. 318), the ultimate ground of the 'destitution' (WPF p. 91) of modernity, of, that is to say, its 'oblivion of Being' (QB p. 318). And metaphysics as a condition of philosophy Heidegger takes to be simply a mirror and articulation of the corresponding condition of our culture. There must, therefore, be something wrong, not with the subject-matter of metaphysics, but with, rather, the way it deals with that subject-matter. Where might this error lie?

In the 'Letter on Humanism' Heidegger says this:

Metaphysics does indeed represent beings in their being, and so it also thinks the being of beings. But it does not think being as such, does not think the difference between being and beings. Metaphysics does not ask about the truth [character?] of being itself. Nor does it therefore ask in what way the essence of human being belongs to the truth of being. (LH p. 246)

This says that metaphysics somehow misconstrues being. It is, Heidegger holds, because of this mistake or 'confusion' concerning the 'ambiguous' phenomenon of 'transcendence' (QB p. 300) that

Being is still waiting for the time when It will become thought-provoking to the human being.[26] (LH p. 246)

What kind of a confusion is it, then, that leads to this 'oblivion of Being'?

14. The crucial failure Heidegger attributes to metaphysics is that of missing, to repeat, '[the] way in which the essence of human being belongs to being'. This accusation is repeated in the passage in which he adopts the startling device of crossing being out: 'B̶e̶i̶n̶g̶' is designed (in its 'negative' role – see p. 16 above), to quote an already quoted passage at greater length, to

prevent . . . the almost ineradicable habit of representing 'being' as something standing somewhere on its own that then on occasion comes face to face with human beings. In accordance with this way of representing matters, it appears as though the human being is excepted from 'being'. However, he is not only not excepted, i.e., not only included in being, but 'being', in needing the human being, is obliged to relinquish this appearance of independence. (QB p. 310)

The crucial truth metaphysics misses is the dependence of being on human being. For short, the 'subjectivity' of being.

Though being is subjective it is very easy to misunderstand the 'ambiguous' nature of this subjectivity, to misunderstand 'in what way' being 'belongs to' human being – and in what way it does not. (I have been guilty of this misunderstanding myself (see HPA pp. 154–5), and Heidegger, too, I strongly suspect, was sometimes confused about the matter.) It is, that is to say, easy to think being, à la Kant, as a set of a priori or 'categorial' features of the objects of our experience which, while characterizing everything within experience, represent nothing that belongs to reality itself. This is how Kant conceives, for instance, space, time and causality. As the 'dottiness' of a newspaper photograph characterizes the photograph but not what it is a photograph of, so space, time and causality characterize all our experience but not what is 'out there', not the real 'in itself'.

Given, however, that being, for Heidegger, is the same as truth (as disclosure), and given the correctness of the explication of Heidegger's account of

---

[26] The justification for my capitalization of 'Being', here, is that the capitalization of 'It' is Heidegger's own.

truth in section 2 above, this is not how the subjectivity of being is to be conceived. Beings, that is to say (to return to our earlier example), are disclosed to us as objects rather than as the surfaces of, or spaces occupied by, those objects. This is a 'categorial' feature of our horizon of disclosure. But it is also a feature of reality itself. Beings *are*, *inter alia*, objects. What is subjective, human-being-dependent, therefore, is not *what* our horizon of disclosure discloses – objectness – but rather the fact that *that particular feature rather than some other* – surfaceness – is disclosed. What is subjective (leaving aside astrology and other such delusions) is not *what* we experience as characterizing reality but rather the *selection* we make from the infinite richness of attributes possessed by reality itself. This is the crucial point made in *Being and Time*'s remark about Newton's Laws (see footnote 5 above). Though the disclosure of reality in terms of Newtonian physics, and therefore our ability to articulate Newton's Laws, was dependent on Newton, *what* is so disclosed is entirely independent of him and of human being in general.

With this clarification of being's 'subjectivity' in mind, let us return to the question of just what it is that constitutes the error of metaphysics, what it is that leads to its failure to see the (in the now-defined sense) subjectivity of being.

In *Identity and Difference*, Heidegger says that we need to take 'the step back', 'the step back out of metaphysics' (ID p. 41; see, too, T p. 181). This suggests that the metaphysician misses something by being, somehow, too 'close up' to things. What he misses is, of course, the phenomenon of disclosure. This is why metaphysics is one and the same error as that of believing there to be no more to truth than correspondence:

metaphysics does not give thought to B/being in its truth, nor does it think such truth as unconcealedness, nor does it think this unconcealedness in its essence. To metaphysics, the essence[27] of truth always appears only in the already derivative form of cognitive knowledge and the truth of propositions that formulate such knowledge. (IWM p. 280)

Once again one needs to be careful to delineate precisely what it is the metaphysician misses in missing the phenomenon of disclosure. At its best at least, to repeat, 'metaphysics does indeed represent beings in their being, and so it also thinks the being of beings': metaphysics does succeed in articulating the categorial, 'universal traits' of reality as we know it. What it misses is

---

[27] In the sense, surely, of *quidditas*, whatness (ET p. 136).

not the being of beings, not being, but rather the fact that that there are just these universal traits which have categorial status for us is dependent on the selection made from the smorgasbord of attributes possessed by reality itself which is made by the linguistic practices, the forms of life, in which we live, and move, and have our being. And missing that, missing, *not* our horizon of disclosure but rather its *horizonal character* – the perspectival character of our basic perspective on things – it elevates its account of the being of beings into *the* (one and only) categorial account of reality itself. Heidegger puts this by saying that, missing the 'fundamental characteristic' of revealing, 'namely revealing as such', the metaphysical interpretation of being 'drives out every other possibility of revealing' (QCT p. 27). Through misunderstanding what it has discovered in discovering the being of beings, it elevates (what is in fact) a particular disclosure to tyrannical status, a status which allows the possibility of no other reality-revealing horizon. I shall refer to this phenomenon as 'absolutization'. As Heidegger uses the term, the error that is metaphysics may be defined as the absolutization of some (of any) horizon of disclosure.

15. What, exactly, is so disastrous about this? Why is it so important to take the 'step back' out of metaphysics?

To absolutize a horizon of disclosure is, to repeat, to 'drive out every other possibility of revealing'. 'Above all', Heidegger continues, 'that revealing which, in the sense of *poiesis*, lets what presences *come forth* into appearance' (QCT p. 27; emphasis mine). This says that the absolutization of a horizon does two things. First, it renders us oblivious to the 'plenitude' of genuine disclosures of reality other than, but concealed by, our own, oblivious to 'the mystery'. Metaphysics blocks access to the 'depth' (compare BT p. 152) and hence sublimity – 'holiness' – of Being. Second, since *poiesis* is the Greek sense of the manifest world as 'brought forth', 'granted' to us in Being's self-disclosing act, the sense of 'nature', in the broadest sense, as the *self*-disclosure of Being (WCT p. 237; see, further, chapter 3 sections 5–6), absolutization renders us oblivious to the '*Es gibt*', to the sense of our world as given to us by the 'It'. Oblivion to disclosure is, *a fortiori*, oblivion to Being's *self*-disclosure.

Metaphysics, then, blocks access to the unfathomable 'depth' of Being, to the mystery of its 'self-concealment', and it blocks access to Being's 'grant-ing' of being to us, to the phenomenon of its self-disclosure, its 'giving' of itself to us (in the *Ereignis*). Metaphysics, therefore, blocks both the mystery of Being and its character as an 'Origin'. Heidegger's phrase 'oblivion of Being', it seems to me, embraces both these effects.

To one gripped by metaphysics, there is, then, no depth and no Origin. Beyond beings, there is – nothing; nothing at all, the abysmal, utterly 'negative', completely 'empty' (BDT p. 151) nothing. This is why Heidegger identifies metaphysics as 'the essence of nihilism' (QB p. 318). Why nihilism, thus literally defined as belief in the nothing, should be a condition of 'destitution', and why it should be the defining condition of modernity (QB p. 318) will be discussed in subsequent chapters.

2   The 'destitution' of modernity

1. The previous chapter offered, in outline, an account of the framework of all of Heidegger's thinking, his 'philosophy of B/being'. It is now time to turn to his discussion, within the context and vocabulary of that framework, of those topics – technology, dwelling, death and ecology, among others – that lend his philosophy existential relevance and urgency.

The physician of culture

Nietzsche once described the philosopher as the 'doctor of culture'. Though Heidegger's taste runs to theological rather than medical metaphors[1] and 'culture' is a word he particularly dislikes,[2] the description is nonetheless apt with respect to his later philosophy. Whereas earlier Heidegger had been concerned (at least officially) with the relatively traditional (Kantian) task of outlining the fundamental structure within which human existence always occurs – a structure common, therefore, to *every* culture – the focus of later Heidegger's thinking is upon the spiritual health of contemporary Western culture.[3] It is this focusing upon *us* that makes later Heidegger more overtly and continuously 'relevant' than earlier Heidegger.

[1] That the theological and the medical are, nonetheless, closely connected for Heidegger is evidenced by his frequent punning on '*heilig*' (holy) and '*heil*' (whole, hale, or healthy). Loss of the *heilig*, he often points out, is loss of the *heil* (WPF p. 141, LH p. 267).

[2] As we have seen, a central Heideggerian position is that historical forms of life are never the product of human intention but are, rather, 'sent' by Being. With respect to such forms of life we are always receptive rather than creative. Coming from the Latin '*cultura*', however, 'culture' implies, Heidegger thinks, 'cultivation', in other words, *self*-cultivation (P p. 70). Further objections to the word concern its elitist connotations and its connotation of something related to the serious business of life in the way that froth is related to beer (see QCT p. 34 and HPA chapter 1 section 6). Though I have some sympathy with all these objections I think it nonetheless possible to use the word, after the manner of many anthropologists, so that it has none of these connotations, and I propose, in fact, to use it quite a lot.

[3] Not *just* Western culture, Heidegger would add. Given the ever-increasing Westernization of every other culture (DL p. 16), Western culture is inexorably achieving 'planetary dominance' (OM p. 72), becoming *the* 'world-civilization' (D p. 140; GA 4 p. 176) (as English is becoming *the* world language).

As with all medical thinking, Heidegger's thinking about the spiritual health of modernity has three essential phases. It begins with an identification of what ails the 'patient' at the symptomatic level, proceeds from there to an identification of the fundamental cause of those symptoms, and from there to the prescription of an appropriate therapy. (Though many critics have effectively suggested there to be no such third phase in later Heidegger's thinking – that he believes there to be nothing we can do about our 'sickness', that 'only a god can save us' – I shall, as I have indicated, be concerned to refute this suggestion.) In this chapter I shall attend to the first phase of this process and then, in a preliminary way, to the second.

2. Many thinkers both lay and professional – perhaps even most of us now that the relative optimism of 'modernism' has given way to the end-of-history nihilism of so-called 'postmodernism' – have sensed that there is something radically amiss with the spiritual condition of the present age. Heidegger possesses this sense to a preeminent degree. Modernity he holds, taking over both the language and sentiment from the early Romantic poet, Friedrich Hölderlin, is the age of the 'world's night', the age, as we have already seen, of 'destitution' (WPF p. 91).[4] What is the character of this destitution?

3. Along with a host of minor symptoms, Heidegger identifies, it seems to me, three major symptoms – or, better, symptom clusters – as the 'essential phenomena' (AWP p. 116) of the sickness, the dis-ease, of modernity. The first I shall call 'loss of the gods', the fact that 'no god any longer . . . disposes the world's history' (WPF p. 91). Since dwelling 'in the sight of the gods . . . is the

---

[4] Historically categorized, Heidegger belongs, together with thinkers such as Ludwig Klages and Ernst Jünger, to what German historians have labelled 'the conservative revolution'. Michael Grossheim has written a fine study which locates Heidegger in relation to other members and factions of this so-called 'revolution' (*Ökologie oder Technokratie?* (Berlin: Dunker und Humblot, 1995)). I, however, because my interest is in the *truth* of Heidegger's 'cultural criticism' rather than its status as an historical-sociological phenomenon, shall not do this. There is, it seems to me, a serious danger pertaining to the historical study of ideas, the danger that the history of ideas becomes the deconstruction of ideas; that once, for example, Heidegger's ideas are positioned on a smorgasbord of similar but also differing and competing options one becomes overwhelmed by the range of choice and the idea that any one set of ideas should be any truer than any other flies out of the window. (Nietzsche called the deliberate deployment of the history of ideas as a technique of devaluation, the 'genealogical' method of 'refutation'.)

ground of the possibility that man can become...a community[5] (GA 39 p. 216), loss of the gods entails, too, loss of community.

The thought here, briefly stated, is the following. The difference between society [*Gesellschaft*] and community [*Gemeinschaft*], as Heidegger explains in section 26 of *Being and Time*, is that whereas the integrity of the former is preserved by nothing more than mutual self-interest, the latter is bound together by common commitment to a shared conception of 'the good life', a shared ethos (see HPA chapter 1 *passim*). This shared ethos, the ethical tradition of a culture ('heritage', in the language of *Being and Time*) is, however, preserved from generation to generation, not in a big book of rules, but by, rather, exemplary, charismatic and therefore authoritative, figures memorialized in the collective memory of the culture. Such figures are what Heidegger calls 'the gods' (see, further, chapter 7 section 6 below). Thus it is that loss of the gods is loss of that which allows a community to be a community. Without them it degenerates into a mere society. *Kultur*, as the Germans sometimes put it, degenerates into mere *Civilization*.

The second and third major symptoms of modernity's dis-ease are, as we will see in chapter 4, both aspects of the loss of what Heidegger calls 'dwelling' – loss of being at home in the world, loss of 'homeliness' in the sense of the German *heimisch* – which Heidegger takes to constitute the 'plight' of modern humanity (BDT p. 161).

The second symptom is modern man's inability to 'own' death (WPF p. 96), the consequence of which, as we will see also in chapter 4, is that our fundamental way of being-in-the-world is anxiety. We are, in a fundamental sense, insecure. Since we cannot own death, and since pain is an intimation of death, we cannot own pain either (*ibid.*).

The third major symptom is, as I shall put it in chapter 3, the 'violence' of modern technology – its violation of both non-human and human nature. Both of these, claims Heidegger, it reduces to 'raw material' for the process of production and consumption, a process which has no purpose other than its own self-perpetuation (OM p. 86, WPF p. 111) – and to fill up the emptiness left by the meaninglessness of modern life (OM p. 86; GA 39 p. 135). Heidegger takes this mindless violence to be unique to Western modernity:

[5] Heidegger actually says 'people [*Volk*]' here. At BT 384, however, he indicates that, for him, 'people' and 'community [*Gemeinschaft*]' are synonyms.

no pre-modern epoch of Western culture exhibited it[6] and neither has any non-Western culture (OM p. 72).

4. There is nothing particularly original about Heidegger's identification of the leading symptoms of modernity's 'sickness'. Nietzsche had discovered the 'death of God', the 'devaluation' of the old Christian values and the subsequent vacuum of 'nihilism', Hegel and Marx had spoken of the 'alienation' of modern humanity, Freud, Rilke and Kafka had identified anxiety as the fundamental mood of modernity, and a whole host of Heidegger's German contemporaries, *inter alios*, Ludwig Klages, Ernst Jünger, Walther Rathenau, The Frankfurt School, E. F. Schumacher, as well as, of course, the contemporary ecological movement (that is to say, most of us to one degree or another) have been appalled by the 'violent' character of modern technology displayed in its effect on both man and nature.

What is original, however – here we move to a preliminary look at the second phase of Heidegger's 'medical' thinking, the identification of the underlying cause of the patient's various ailments – is Heidegger's deployment of his 'philosophy of B/being' to provide an account of the underlying cause of each of the symptom clusters mentioned above. The fundamental cause of each is, he claims, 'metaphysics', the absolutization of a horizon of disclosure (*which* horizon we do not yet know), its misinterpretation as, not one reality-disclosing horizon among many, but rather as, uniquely, *the* structure of reality itself. From this it follows – to glance briefly toward the therapeutic phase of Heideggerian thinking – that the recovery of our culture from its present destitution, the 'turning' from modernity to an authentically postmodern age, will consist, above all, in 'overcoming metaphysics' (OM p. 67). This use of his *Seinsphilosophie* to diagnose and describe the fundamental cause of the widely recognized symptoms of modernity's lack of health lends to Heidegger's thinking, it seems to me, a profundity matched by no other physician of modernity.

---

[6] There is a problem about the Romans. Sometimes Heidegger characterizes their 'imperial' disposition in very much the same terms of violence as he characterizes modernity. Sometimes there is a suggestion the transition to violence was the transition from Greece to Rome. Mainly, however, Heidegger thinks of violent technology as beginning with the modern age, and more specifically, with the Industrial Revolution (for example, at QCT p. 5).

Loss of the gods

5. Heidegger's claim that 'metaphysics' is the single underlying cause of all of the symptoms of disease mentioned above is an extraordinarily ambitious attempt to bring unity out of a seemingly disparate plurality. And it is not, in general, at all obvious that the claim is true, or even plausible. In the case of the gods,[7] however, the connexion between their loss, on the one hand, and metaphysics, on the other, the question as to why a metaphysical disclosure of reality must drive the gods away, is relatively easy to answer and may be dealt with straight away.

Heidegger says that the loss of the gods is a sign and consequence of something 'even grimmer': the extinction of 'the divine radiance...in the world's history' (WPF p. 91), of, that is to say, 'the holy', that 'aether in which alone the gods are gods' (WPF p. 94). Gods are, by definition, holy. They appear 'out of the holy sway' (BDT p. 150), are radiantly charismatic. Living gods, as we will see in chapter 7 (section 6), are figures which inspire us to live according to the fundamental ethos of our community. This is why they must be radiant. To be authoritative – by way of charisma rather than force – they must stand out as 'remove[d] from any comparison' with other beings' (T p. 178). Christ, for example, must 'shine' to inspire one to the Christian life. (In most Christian iconography, of course, encircled by a golden halo, he quite literally shines.) But modernity has lost its sense of the holy *in general*, Heidegger claims (WPF p. 117). That 'no god any longer gathers men and things unto himself, visibly and unequivocally, and by such gathering disposes the world's history and man's sojourn in it' (WPF p. 91), that no god any longer shapes the life of our culture as a whole – and thereby the lives of the individuals who belong to it – is a symptom of the world's *general* loss of radiance. That (unlike ancient Greek, Polynesian, Aboriginal or Mbuti culture) our culture no longer responds to nature as a sacred place, that it no longer responds to it as, in the words of *Being and Time*, that 'which 'stirs and strives', which assails us and enthralls us as landscape' (BT 70), is another symptom of the same phenomenon.

[7] Heidegger's Being is, I have suggested, 'God'. But it is extremely important not to confuse this 'God' with what Heidegger refers to as 'the gods' or sometimes 'the divinities'. The latter are beings; the former, of course, is not. For a full discussion of 'the gods' see chapter 7 sections 6–7.

But loss of radiance, *Entzauberung*, dis-enchantment, to use the term Max Weber used to identify what he took to be the defining characteristic of modernity,[8] is a necessary consequence of metaphysics. If, that is to say, we absolutize our horizon of disclosure then we become oblivious to the unfathomable depth of Being, oblivious to our world as the self-disclosing gift of the infinitely self-concealing. Instead of the mystery of the 'globe of Being', reality is reduced to (in every sense of the word) a flat, illuminated disk. Instead of something awesome and astonishing, an object of 'wonder' (GA 52 p. 64), the world 'obtrudes . . . in a dry, monotonous and therefore oppressive way' (QCT p. 17). It loses its magic, becomes dis-enchanted. Notice that, following in Schopenhauer's footsteps, Heidegger here identifies a kind of *boredom* as the characteristic mood of modernity. (One of his striking insights is that cultures as well as individuals have moods.) Whereas Pre-Socratic Greece was an ecstatic culture modernity is bored.

6. It is, then, relatively easy to understand how metaphysics and the 'oblivion of Being' it entails is the underlying ground of modernity's loss of the gods[9] (and why recovery of the sacred is a precondition for their return). With respect to the other two leading symptoms of modernity's distress, however, the connexion is by no means so easy to establish. In the next chapter I shall attend to the question of why metaphysics is the underlying ground of modern technology, and in chapter 4 to the question of why it is the underlying ground of modernity's 'homelessness' (BDT p. 161).

---

[8] There are no longer, wrote Weber, any 'mysterious, incalculable forces that come into play, but rather . . . one can, in principle, master all things by calculation. This means that the world is disenchanted' (*Max Weber: Essays in Sociology*, trans. H. H. Gerth and C. Wright Mills (New York: Oxford University Press, 1958), p. 139).

[9] Another way of saying that metaphysics is the ground of loss of the gods is to say that it is loss of that 'God' which I argued, in chapter 1, to be identical with Heidegger's 'Being', that is the ground of our loss of the gods. It is very important, however, not to confuse 'God' in this sense with either 'the gods' or with the God of traditional Christian theology.

3   The essence of modern technology

1. As we saw in chapter 1, an 'essence', in one of Heidegger's central senses, is a 'ground' that 'enables' (ET p. 136). In this sense, we saw, being is the essence of beings: it makes them possible as the beings they are in the way that the visual field makes visual objects possible. This is the sense of 'essence' uppermost in 'The Question concerning Technology', the 1949 essay (revised in 1955) that represents the most considered statement of Heidegger's philosophy of technology. As there understood, the essay explains, the 'essence' of something is that in virtue of which it 'holds sway' and 'endures' (QCT p. 30). It is, in other words, the underlying ground, explanation or cause of the phenomenon of which it is the 'essence'. It is in this sense that Heidegger wishes to maintain that metaphysics – the absolutization of a horizon of disclosure – is the essence of modern technology. That he wishes also to claim that something which he calls '*das Gestell*' ('Enframing', in its standard translation) is the essence of modern technology means that we will need to look for some kind of coincidence of meaning between 'metaphysics' and '*das Gestell*'.

Before seeking to understand Heidegger's claim(s) about the underlying explanatory ground of modern technology we need, first, to understand the nature of the explanandum. We need, that is, to understand what that character or nature is which, in Heidegger's view, makes modern Western technology unique, different from that of every other culture and every other epoch in the history of the West.

Ancient technology

2. Heidegger's characterization of modern technology proceeds *via* a contrast between modern, on the one hand, and pre-modern – paradigmatically Greek – technology on the other.

Compare and contrast 'the old wooden bridge' (QCT p. 16) that 'lets the river run its course' (BDT p. 152) with the modern hydro-electric dam that turns it into a reservoir. Or the ancient peasant farm where the farmer 'places the seed in the keeping of the forces of growth' (QCT p. 15) with the modern mono-cultural, artificially fertilized, E.U.-subsidized, mechanized (and so countryside depopulating) branch of 'the mechanized food industry' (*ibid.*). Or compare the ancient woodcutter who took the wood he needed but allowed the forest to remain the forest, with the modern timber company which clear-fells the native forest, and replants with exotic pines whose acid needles make it impossible that anything else should grow. It seems that whereas ancient technology existed in harmonious and respectful rapport with nature, modern technology constitutes a kind of 'setting upon' (QCT p. 16), a rape or violation of nature. Whereas ancient technology was, as we may put it, 'gentle', modern technology is, to use E. F. Schumacher's term, 'violent technology'.[1]

3. It is very important to see that, characterized in this way, 'technology' must mean, for Heidegger, technological *practice*. Though he himself is somewhat confused about this – at one point he suggests the ancient-modern contrast to be a contrast between handwork and machine technology (QCT p. 5) – the ancient-modern contrast cannot be a contrast between handtools and machines but rather between what we *do* with technological devices, regardless of whether they be tools or machines. Though some modern machines and technological systems – the hydrogen bomb and factories that reduce human beings to automata – are inherently violent, there is no logical impossibility in the thought of using the fruits of modern scientific and technological knowledge in the 'gentle' way Heidegger takes to characterize traditional practice, no logical impossibility in the coming into being, in modernity, of what Schumacher calls 'intermediate' and I (more felicitously, I think) 'gentle' technology. And neither is there any logical guarantee that if we use traditional hand-tools we will use them in the gentle manner in which they were supposedly used in the past. One can be just as violent with a spade as with a bulldozer – it just takes longer and occurs, therefore, on a reduced scale. But even the scale of violation produced by traditional means can sometimes rival that produced by modern. All it takes to destroy a rain forest is fire.

[1] *Small is Beautiful* (Sphere: London, 1974) *passim.*

4. Before proceeding to search for the ground of the violence of modern technology it will be as well to ask for the ground of the 'gentleness' of Greek technology. This is likely to prove an important guide as to how we need to become to overcome the violence of our current relationship to things.

The heart of any kind of technology is causation. In its modern conception, Heidegger points out, causation is *making happen*; in the most important kind of human causation it is 'manufacturing [*machen*]'. The ancient conception, on the other hand, is something quite different. Causation, for the Greeks, is a matter of 'bringing forth'; 'bringing forth out of concealment into unconcealment', 'letting what is not yet present arrive in its presencing' (QCT pp. 10–11). Thus, extrapolating from Aristotle's record of the Greek conception of 'the four causes', the ancient silversmith, in making a silver chalice, 'considers carefully and gathers together', first, silver, the matter or 'material cause' of the chalice, second, the 'aspect' or '*eidos*' of the chalice, its design or 'formal cause', and third, the human social practice of sacrifice and worship for which the chalice is to provide the centrepiece, the vessel's *telos* or 'final cause', its purpose. In his 'pondering' of these elements, says Heidegger, the silversmith 'brings forth' what is implicit in them (QCT pp. 6–9). The same is true of the ancient cabinet maker who, he says, required himself to 'answer and respond to all the different kinds of wood and the shapes slumbering within the wood as it enters into man's dwelling with the hidden riches of nature' (WCT p. 14).

One place where the idea of 'bringing forth' survives into modernity is in the fine arts. In particular, sculptors familiarly describe themselves, as Heidegger describes the cabinet maker, as 'releasing' the figure already 'slumbering' in the marble. If we compare sensitive sculpture with the manufacture of, say, aluminium beer cans, we obtain a vivid sense of the distinction between the manufacturing of modernity and the bringing forth of the Greeks that Heidegger is trying to draw.

(One difficulty which might occur to one at this point is that in the sculptor's marble or the cabinet maker's wood there 'slumbers' no *unique* figure. There are, obviously, many figures the sculptor may produce from a given piece of marble without in any way compromising her artistic competence or integrity. How, then, one might ask, can Heidegger speak as if there were such a thing as bringing forth *the* figure implicit in the wood, *the* chalice implicit in matter, form, and social practice?

The answer, I think, is that though no unique figure is determined by (for short) the given, a limited range of figures is so determined. If a figure lies within that range it is 'brought forth', if not, a 'violation' of the given occurs. (In sculpture, a figure that violates its materials usually breaks.) The illuminating analogy, here, is with, I think, the performance artwork. Though there is no definitive performance of a Beethoven symphony – great art, as great, is too multifaceted for that – the work nonetheless imposes limits outside which a performance is no longer a performance of that work but rather its violation. Baz Luhrmann's (unfortunately influential) text-terrified, poetry-killing transportation of *Romeo and Juliet* into the urban debris of a gun-crazed Los Angeles springs to mind as a prime example of such a violation.)

5. Greek technology was, then, the gentleness of 'bringing forth' rather than the violence of making happen. What, however, to repeat the question, is the ground of this gentleness?

Heidegger says: 'he who ... knows what is knows what he wills in the midst of what is' (OWA p. 67). This conveys his fundamental thought: how you (roughly speaking) see things is how you act. The character of a culture's fundamental horizon of disclosure is the 'essence', the explanatory ground, of the fundamental character of its action. How, then, did the Greeks see things?

Heidegger's entry into the ancient disclosure of B/being is *via* language (QCT pp. 10–13). The Greek word for 'bringing forth' is, he observes, *poiesis*. This divides into two kinds. First, unaided bringing forth as, for example, the 'bursting of a blossom into bloom'. This is *physis*, the Greek word for nature. Second, aided bringing forth in which the craftsman, or 'technician', lends a hand to nature's 'blossoming' (SR p. 160). This is what the Greeks called *techne*.

Heidegger often stresses that the modern distinction between the productive crafts and the fine arts was foreign to the Greeks, that for them, artists were as much 'technicians' as craftsmen. And the same for thinkers. The Greeks, he says, included 'the arts of the mind' as a species of the bringing forth of *techne* (QCT p. 13). (The 'Socratic' method of teaching, and the construction of a state that articulates the ethos if its 'people' come to mind as thinkerly 'bringings forth'.)

6. The Greek understanding of the relationship between natural and human activity looked, then, like this:

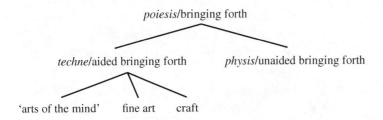

poiesis/bringing forth

techne/aided bringing forth   *physis*/unaided bringing forth

'arts of the mind'   fine art   craft

The question remains, however, as to *why* they saw their own activities as – when conducted in a 'fitting' (I p. 82) manner – continuous in the above way with the activities of nature, why they saw their own, in the broadest sense, 'building' as continuous with nature's own 'building'. (In 'The Thing' Heidegger refers to 'earth' as 'the building bearer' (T p. 178).) Why, in short, was the above scheme normative for the Greeks?

The model for *poiesis* is, we saw, the blossom rising forth out of its bud. The blossoming of (let us say) a rose is something that happens *within* nature. At its most fundamental level, however, *poiesis* is the blossoming forth *of* nature. The sense of the visible world as a whole as *poiesis* is the sense of it as a blossoming forth, an 'upsurgent presencing' (ET p. 145) out of, as it were (though Heidegger himself does not put it this way), the 'world bud'. The two 'buds' are, of course, very different. Whereas the rose bud is visible and known, the 'world bud' is utterly mysterious, incomprehensible. And in the majesty of its overwhelming creative power, it is breathtakingly 'awesome' (OWA p. 68).

The Greeks, then, experienced their world as brought into, and sustained in, being by an overwhelmingly powerful, utterly mysterious force. More exactly, they experienced it as the self-display of the simultaneously self-concealing divinity, 'the most sublime of gods' (I p. 58), as Sophocles calls it. But this made the Greek world a place pregnant with the presence of 'the overpowering' (IM p. 150), 'touched by the exciting nearness of the fire from the heavens' (GA 39 p. 292). It was, in short, a numinous world, a holy, a sacred place.

With respect to technology this had two consequences. First, since the fundamental order of things is a divine – the divinity's – order, one's stance to it is one, not of violence, but of, rather, respect and reverence; 'sparing and preserving' (BDT p. 149). Towards the major, structural features of the divinity's self-expression[2] (its performance artwork, as one might be inclined to think of it), towards great rivers, forests, mountains as well as human communities and life-forms ('peoples'), technological activity will always be circumscribed by fundamental considerations of conservation. Second, insofar as one's being in the world is a matter of making changes rather than conserving things as they are, then, rather than the violence of 'making', it will be the 'gentleness' of 'letting what is coming arrive'. Better put, it is a matter of allowing the divine 'Origin' (I *passim*, OWA p. 60,[3] DK p. 212) of things to complete its self-disclosure through one's own creative activities. (See further, chapters 7 and 8 below.)

In a word, then, the 'gentleness' of the Greeks lay in the fact that the world disclosed itself to them as a holy place.

7. Before proceeding to the question of the ground of the violence of modern technological practice it will be as well to confront an objection invariably raised against Heidegger's account of the Greeks, particularly by those eager to discount his critique of the present: the objection that he *sentimentalizes* them. In reality, the criticism runs, far from being the Arcadian bunch of 'Greens' of Heidegger's dream, the Greeks were very like us. To the extent that our technological activity amounts to the exploitation and violation of human and non-human nature, so, too, did theirs. To pretend otherwise is mere alienation from the present, nothing more than nostalgia.

Various points could be made here. One could ask for evidence of the supposed universality of human, technological nature. And, against such a thesis, one could point to the powerful array of linguistic evidence Heidegger assembles in support of his claim that the Greeks understood nature and their own proper technological relationship to it in a way fundamentally different from the way we do. (Only a fraction of this has been touched on in the foregoing discussion.) It is possible, of course, that this evidence is selectively

---

[2] In a passage quoted and discussed by Heidegger, Hölderlin calls the unified structure of such features the 'thought' which underlies nature (see GA 4 pp. 50–60).

[3] The translator's word, here, is 'reservoir'. But Heidegger's is *Herkunftsbereich*, 'originating region'.

chosen and that one could point to other evidence, both linguistic[4] and non-linguistic[5], which suggests the Greeks to have had a technological relationship to things very like ours. The main point to be made, however, is very simple, namely, that it matters not at all to Heidegger's essential purpose, whether his 'Greeks' are actual or fictional (or, as seems most likely, somewhere in between). The reason for their introduction, that is to say, is twofold. First, to provide an antipode in contrast to which the violence of modern technological practice will be clearly apparent. And second, to provide an intimation of the kind of world-experience necessary to a technological practice that is gentle rather than violent. This purpose Heidegger's 'Greeks' can serve even if they are *entirely* fictional. All that is required is that 'Greek' technology – as both practice and underlying world-disclosure – be a *possible* technology, not that it be actual. Like Martin Luther King's dream, Heidegger's dream, even if

---

[4] One passage that comes to mind is the first chorus from Sophocles' *Antigone* quoted often enough by Heidegger himself (for example, at I pp. 58–9):

> Manifold and uncanny, yet nothing
> more uncanny looms or stirs beyond the human being
> He ventures forth on the foaming tide
> amid the southern storm of winter
> and crosses the surge
> of cavernous waves.
> And the most sublime of gods, the earth,
> indestructible and untirring, he wears out.
> turning the soil from year to year,
> working the ploughs to and fro
> with his horses.
>
> And the flock of birds that rises into the air
> he ensnares ...
> He overpowers with cunning the animal
> ... the never-tamed bull ...
> he forces under the yoke.

Notice, however, that the passage seems to be a *pathology* of the human being, a 'Green' critique of the way the Greeks practised technology at least some of the time. There is no suggestion Sophocles *endorses* the 'wearing out' of 'the most sublime of gods'.

[5] For example the facts that Greek culture was based on slavery and that the deforestation of the Greek countryside began in antiquity. Both of these phenomena are too complex to be properly investigated here. I wish only to suggest that, in the main, the Greeks denied slaves the rights of citizens for the same reason they denied children those rights – their slaves they saw as infantile and as, therefore, *appropriately* treated as slaves. (What they missed, like the Americans of the Deep South, is that infantilism (Uncle-Tomism) is the *product* of slavery rather than the other way round.) On the seriously exaggerated nature of the claim about deforestation see Joachim Rodkau, *Natur und Macht. Ein Weltgeschichte der Umwelt* (Munich: Beck, 2000) pp. 160–4.

it is *only* a dream, can show us the deficiencies of our present and point us towards a gentler future.

Modern technology

8. The salient characteristic of modern technology is, then, violence. This perception is by no means unique to Heidegger. It was shared by many of his contemporaries such as Ludwig Klages and Ernst Jünger, by, as we have seen, E. F. Schumacher, and by, of course, contemporary ecological thinking in general; to one degree or another, that is to say, by most of us. What is, however, unique to Heidegger, is his account of the 'essence', the fundamental ground, of the violence of modern technology.

As already remarked, Heidegger calls this ground '*das Gestell*' (the meaning of which, remember, has to coincide with the meaning of 'metaphysics'). Lovitt's translation of this as 'Enframing' is, for at least two reasons, a poor one. The first is that it makes *das Gestell* look like a human action (ensnaring, encoding, enveloping) whereas, in reality, as we will see, it is not an action but rather a mode of disclosure which determines the character of action. The second is that it misses out the definite article, '*das*', thereby disguising the fact that the phrase is a proper name (or 'definite description' in philosophers' jargon) designating, not something that can happen in any age or culture, but, uniquely, the 'essence' of Western modernity. (Though Lovitt tries to compensate by capitalizing the 'E' this device is (a) easy to forget and (b), given all the other capitals floating around in Heidegger, of uncertain force.) Since '*Gestell*' means, in ordinary German 'frame', 'rack', 'shelf' or 'stand', and '*stellen*' means to 'set' or 'place', a better translation might be something like 'the frame-up'. I, however, propose to save space and trees by leaving '*Gestell*' untranslated and taking the presence of the definite article to be always implicitly understood.

9. What is *Gestell*? Heidegger says it is that epoch-defining – Western modernity defining – horizon of disclosure according to which 'the real reveals itself as *Bestand*' (QCT p. 23). Lovitt translates '*Bestand*' by means of the neologism 'standing-reserve'. This does not accord with Heidegger's practice which is to take a familiar word and extend its meaning into unfamiliar territory. In ordinary German '*Bestand*' means 'stock' or 'supply'. Heidegger,

however, uses it to cover not only those things of which one might have a stock or supply – oil, electricity, timber – but also the machines – the 'airliner that stands on the runway' (QCT p. 17) – that are powered by or operate upon those things. I shall mimic this procedure by taking the ordinary word 'resource' and extending it to cover not just the substances that power and are transformed by machines but also the machines themselves. Not just machines but also bureaucratic, machine-like entities: the modern university, for example, in which one finds no longer teachers and students but rather 'suppliers' and 'consumers' and everything which that entails. (Compare Heidegger on the 'supply' of health consumers to the modern hospital (QCT p. 18).)

Remembering that Heidegger sometimes calls the mode of disclosure which defines an epoch its 'ontology' (or 'metaphysics' in his non-pejorative sense), we might attempt to say what *Gestell* is by defining it as that horizon of disclosure according to which

(1) to be is to be an item of resource

– something, that is, which is available for productive activity, something, in the language of *Being and Time*, 'ready-to-hand'. Modern technological practice, so the idea would then run, is uniquely violent because modernity is the age in which reality discloses itself in such a way that for an entity to be in being is for it to be an item of resource.

Obviously, however, (1) is totally implausible as an account of the ontology of modernity, or of any age, since it makes no mention of the beings to whom resources are available, the owners of the 'hands' to which things are 'ready'. It fails to mention, that is, that second major category in terms of which *Being and Time* analyses the life-world, '*Dasein*', the human being. With this in mind we might then seek to modulate (1) into

(2) to be is to be either an object available for productive activity or else a subject who makes use of such objects in such activity.

This, however, will not capture Heidegger's understanding of *Gestell* either. The reason is that the subject-object formulation makes it look as though the human being stands outside the realm of resource, of the things that are manipulated and exploited in productive activity, that it reigns over the 'global' (IM p. 199)[6] productive mechanism as its lord and master (compare

---

[6] Notice that 'globalization' was an issue for Heidegger already in 1935.

QCT p. 27). A fundamental Heideggerian insight, however – one which he shared, not only with German contemporaries such as Klages and Jünger but with, I would suggest, most of us – is that this is an illusion. While the subject-object picture may have possessed a certain accuracy with respect to early modernity, the truth about mature modernity (that which we misleadingly call 'postmodernity') is that, like the broom of Goethe's sorcerer's apprentice (see S p. 105) or *2001*'s HAL, the machine that was supposed to be our slave has become instead our master. Human being has lost its apartness, has itself become part of the to-be-exploited, has become, as contemporary language – modernity's 'house of being' – indeed tells us, 'human resource [*Material*]' (QCT p. 18, WPF p. 111). (Notice that Heidegger was sensitive to this change in language already in 1946.)

Of course human beings are 'the most important raw material' (OM p. 86) (for which reason Heidegger predicts – in 1966 – that 'some day factories will be built for the artificial breeding of human material . . . according to plan and need' (*ibid*)).[7] They are the most important because as well as being available for manipulation and exploitation as productive units they are also the manipulators and exploiters, as it were the portals through which the global system of production and consumption – a system which, to repeat, is circular and so pointless – maintains itself.

To capture the idea that, in the world of *Gestell*, humans are, on the one hand resource, but on the other uniquely valuable, we need to distinguish 'first' and 'second order' resources: first order resources, let us say, are those which are *just* objects of productive activity, second order resources are those which are *both* objects *and* subjects of productive activity. Using this distinction we might, then, modulate (2) into

(3) to be is to be either a first or second order resource.

10. Actually, however, this still fails to do the job of capturing that mode of world-disclosure unique to modernity and, as such, capable of explaining the unique character of modern technological practice. The reason is that, first, it is not merely modern but rather *any* technological practice that requires the

---

[7] This was Heidegger's perception of Nazi eugenics and Nazi racism: that 'the organization of a nation's vital resouces and race' (IM p. 47) was a visible sign of the ever-widening dominion of *Gestell*, of the transformation of the human being into human resource. (See, further, HPN chapter 1 section 16, and chapter 6 section 7.)

disclosure of the world as resource and, second, technological practice is a *universal* feature of human existence. Formula (3), in short, so I am about to argue, describes something that belongs to the 'ontology' of *every* epoch of human history and cannot, therefore, identify that 'essence' which is unique to modernity.

11. Heidegger understands the notion of technological practice, in other words 'work', in a 'broad and multifarious' (WPF p. 110) way – 'ontologically' rather than 'ontically', in the language of *Being and Time*. According to this understanding, 'work' means something like 'intentional production (or attempted production) of a change in the world'. Heideggerian 'work' does not, then, mean 'paid employment' and is not in any way opposed to 'leisure'.

Man, says Heidegger, is essentially the being that works, the being that 'produces' things (WPF p. 110). Heidegger's word, here, is *herstellen*. This is the ordinary German word for 'manufacture' but divided by a hyphen into its etymological components – *her-stellen* – it means 'to place here; to place here before us in thought, that is to say to represent. Heidegger puns on the two meanings of *herstellen* (one can perform the same trick with the Latin origin of 'pro-duce') to mark the intimate link that exists between production and representation. Thus when Heidegger says that man is essentially the being who 'produces' he means something like: the human being is essentially that being which (a) represents the world as it is (b) represents the world as it wills it to be and (c) 'calculates' the course of action required to bridge the gap.[8] Work in this broad sense is not only essential but also unique to the human being: 'animals and all beings that merely exist cannot work' (LS, p. 54).

Not only are human beings (of every epoch and culture) *essentially* and uniquely workers, they are almost *always* workers. Work, in Heidegger's broad sense, is not just a, but rather *the*, central feature of human existence, its 'everydayness' (GA 52 p. 65). Save when we sleep, we are almost always pro-ducing, almost always, in one way or another, at work. This is the reason *Being and Time*'s life-world, the world of 'average everydayness', defined, as it is, in terms of equipment, the users of equipment, and the users of the

---

[8] That Heidegger thinks, as we saw in chapter 1 (section 10), that 'calculative thinking' is what human beings do nearly all of the time corresponds to (what we are about to see to be) his view that what they do nearly all of the time is work.

products of such use, is very obviously *identical with* the work-world. Dealing with equipment is, says Heidegger, 'the way in which everyday Dasein *always* is' (BT 67; my emphasis).

The human being as such is, then, essentially, uniquely, and almost always a worker, a technological being engaged in technological activity. But (the first thinker clearly to articulate this point was Arthur Schopenhauer) work requires that things are represented, that they show up, in work-suitable, 'ready-to-hand', instrumental, technological ways. This was as true for the Greeks as it is for us. You cannot build a temple unless things show up as first order resources, unless the hillside shows as a quarry of stone, the land as a building site, and the piece of metal as a chisel. And you cannot organize the building of a temple unless your masons, sculptors and painters show up as second order resource. The ancient Greek – to change the example – could not have bought shoes unless the cobbler showed up as a human resource, Phaedrus could not have learnt rhetoric had Socrates not showed up (though Phaedrus would not have put it this way) as a relevant kind of 'information resource'.

Heidegger clearly acknowledges this Schopenhauerian point. Because he is necessarily and almost always 'at work', the world as he experiences it is 'twisted around[9] towards the human being' (WPF p. 110), shows up, that is, under technological descriptions. Note that Heidegger says, here, '*the* human being', not 'the modern human being'.

Let us call the disclosure of things as (first and second order) resource 'the technological disclosure of B/being'. Note that there are *many* modes of the technological disclosure of B/being: the disclosure that grounded Greek handicraft technology was different from that which grounds machine technology. And the disclosure which grounds cybernetic technology represents a still further difference. Again, the disclosure which governs everyday technological action in the 'life-world' – the disclosure of things as shoes and ships and cabbages and kings – is different from the technological world-disclosure

---

[9] *Verdreht.* 'Twisted' has a pathological ring to it which is odd given that Heidegger is describing, here, the world-disclosure of, not degenerate modern man, but rather humanity as such. The explanation is that at this point he is inhabiting the Rilkean lament that, unlike (according to Rilke) the animals (or, one might add, the supposedly 'intuitive' intelligence of Kant's God), our access to 'the Open' (Being) is impeded by representation, by, in other words, language. Sometimes Heidegger inhabits the frame of mind which sees language as a tragic burden, a kind of cage which, if it does not completely cut us off from access to Being, at least makes the achievement of that access problematic in a way in which it is not for more 'innocent' beings.

provided by sub-atomic physics. (Heidegger argues compellingly, as we will see, that modern natural science *is* a technological world-disclosure, that it is governed by the imperative to present reality not as it is 'in itself', but to present it, rather, in ways that are 'workable'.)

What the above reflections on the (double) universality of work and of the disclosure of the world in work-suitable ways mean is that *every* epoch of human history has its technological disclosure of B/being – including that of 'the Greeks'. But this means that the disclosure of the world as resource – its resource-ful disclosure, as I shall be inclined to put it – is compatible with, indeed *essential to*, 'gentle' as much as it is to 'violent' technological practice. So the statement that modernity is the age in which technology is grounded in things showing up as (first and second order) resource does nothing to explain the difference between our technological practice and that of other ages and cultures. Unless Heidegger's thinking about technology is totally inadequate, therefore, there must be more to *Gestell* than is captured even by our twice-revised attempt to explain what it is. Otherwise put, 'the real's revealing itself as resource' can be only one aspect of *Gestell*. There must be more to it than has so far met the eye. What more?

12. What Heidegger in fact says (for expository purposes I earlier suppressed part of the quotation) is: 'what *Gestell* itself actually is . . . is the way [*Weise*] in which the real reveals itself as resource' (QCT p. 23). This talk of 'ways' suggests that there is more than one way in which resource-ful world-disclosure can occur and that the essence of modern technology lies in a *particular* way. What might this be?

Heidegger says that in the age of *Gestell* 'what is unconcealed no longer concerns man even as object, but does so, rather, *exclusively* as resource' (QCT p. 27; my emphasis). This suggests that while beings show up in every age as resource, the 'way' they show up that is unique to modernity is as *pure* resource, *nothing but* resource. So, as a fourth attempt to explicate *Gestell*, we might say that modernity is the epoch in which world-disclosure is such that

(4) to be is to be *nothing but* (first or second order) resource.

That this formula finally succeeds in hitting the nail on the head is confirmed by Heidegger's well-known image of the world's showing up to modernity as 'a gigantic petrol station' (DT p. 50), the point about petrol stations being not that they are resources but rather that they are *nothing but* resources. There is *nothing to them* other than their resource-fulness, no being other than their being-as-resource. Petrol stations are, in a certain sense, one-dimensional places (which, to anticipate, has something to do with their charmlessness).

13. Why, thus understood, should *Gestell* constitute the explanatory ground of the violence of modern technology? What the emphasis on the 'nothing but' suggests is that while in earlier ages things showed up as resource *plus* something else, modernity has lost this 'plus' and that this is why its relation to beings has decayed into violence. What, we need now to ask, is the nature of this 'plus'?

Heidegger says that when *Gestell* 'holds sway'

it drives out every other possibility of revealing. Above all, *Gestell* conceals that revealing which, in the sense of *poiesis*, lets what presences come forth into appearance.

'As compared with this other order' of *poiesis*, Heidegger continues, *Gestell* 'thrusts' man into an 'antithetical' relation to things, the relation of 'setting upon' (QCT p. 27). These remarks suggest that there are two aspects to the 'plus' that *Gestell* excludes: a revealing of things in which they show up other than as pure resource, and the revealing that is *poiesis*. I shall discuss these in turn.

14. What revealings of beings are there other than as pure resource? Heidegger says, to repeat, that 'when destining reigns in the mode of *Gestell*', when *Gestell* achieves world-historical, epoch-defining status, 'what is unconcealed no longer concerns man even as object' (QCT pp. 26–7). Whereas in pre-modern times man inhabited a world of 'objects', in modernity, 'even the object disappears into the objectlessness of [pure] resource' (QCT p. 19). In modernity, says Heidegger, beings 'no longer stand [*stand*] over against [*gegen*] us as object [*Gegenstand*]' with the result that everything shows up as 'completely unautonomous' (QCT p. 17).

It is important to notice that 'object', for Heidegger, is not *opposed to* 'resource'. Objects *are* resources. When a being (to quote a little more of the passage quoted on page 48 above) 'becomes an object [it] . . . is thereby twisted around towards the human being' for technological purposes, purposes of 'production' (WPF p. 110). What, then, is the difference between the resource-ful way things show up in modernity and the resource-ful way they showed up in pre-modern times when things – at least some of them[10] – showed up as objects?

'Completely unautonomous' suggests a contrast with 'partially unauto-nomous'. Objects are partially unautonomous because, I suggest, as resources, they show up under descriptions that are dependent on us and our work-practices. Were there to be no carpenters there could be no hammers. Were there to be no masons there could be no quarries (though there might be heaps) of stone. But objects are partially 'autonomous' too.[11] When things show up as objects they show up, says Heidegger, in their 'essence' in the sense of 'ownness [*Eigentlichkeit*]' (GA 52 pp. 65–6). This is to say, I suggest, that they show up in that *quidditas*, 'whatness' (ET p. 136), or nature which they have independently of us and our practices.[12] So, *qua* object, while a being shows up as resource, and is, to that extent, 'unautonomous', it *also* shows up in the nature which it has independently of us. We can put the matter as follows. When things show up as objects they show up in their, as I shall say, 'being-for-us'. But they show up, too, in their 'being-in-itself', that 'ownness' they have independently of us.[13] When, for example, the West coast of New Zealand's South Island shows up as object it shows up not only as a stand of timber but also as a forest of indigenous and unique beech trees.

In driving out objectness, therefore, what *Gestell* deprives us of is the being-in-itself of things. Things show up *exclusively* in terms of their being-for-us.

---

[10] See footnote 13 below.

[11] Heidegger is not always consistent about this. In the 1938 'The Age of the World Picture', for example, it is clear that 'object' has precisely the meaning of 'pure resource'. The more thoughtful use of the term seems to begin during the 1940s.

[12] That a world of beings is disclosed at all is, we have seen, dependent on us and our 'linguistic' practices. Surely, then, it may be objected, there are *no* properties which things have indepen-dently of us and our practices. This, however, is a mistaken objection. That, to repeat (see chapter 1 footnote 5), the *medium* of disclosure is dependent on us and our practices does not entail that *what* is disclosed is so dependent. The great pianist's interpretation of a Beethoven piano sonata, a performance which, perhaps, discloses some novel facet of the music, is dependent on the pianist. But what it discloses – if the performance is a truly great one – was in the music all along.

[13] As Heidegger points out (QCT p. 17), not everything *can* show up as an object, the reason being that some things have no being-in-itself distinct from their being-for-us. With tools and machines, human artifacts in general, their nature or 'whatness' *is* their being-for-us. A way of describing *Gestell* is to say that it discloses *everything* as a tool or machine, a point captured by the 'gigantic petrol station' (DT p. 50) image.

15. The second aspect of beings excluded by *Gestell*, as we saw, is *poiesis*. The character of what is excluded we already know. The world shows up as *poiesis*, we saw (section 5 above), when it shows up as a holy place, the self-disclosure of the awesomely incomprehensible 'Origin' of things. Heidegger has various ways of describing this way of the world's showing up. Sometimes he calls it 'the *Ereignis*' (Event, with a capital 'E') or '*Ereignis*-experience', experience of 'transport and enchantment [*Entrückung und Berückung*]' (GA 65 p. 70). At other times he calls it 'the thing's thinging' (which, because a thing is inseparable from the context of world which makes it the thing that it is, is also 'the world's worlding' (T pp. 177–82)). Things 'thing' (*dingen*, a neologism which, not accidentally, rhymes with *singen*, to sing) when they show up as radiant, charismatic, sacred beings. A 'thing' in Heidegger's especially elevated use of the term, is something that is disposed to thing. Though, in modernity, they hardly ever exercise this disposition, *everything* is, in fact, a 'thing' (a 'deep' tautology), even the humblest: 'the jug and the bench, the footbridge and the plough, . . . tree and pond, too, brook and hill, are things each in its own way' (T p. 182). Using this terminology of the 'thing' we can express the second exclusion exercised by *Gestell*, the exclusion of *poiesis*, by saying that what it 'drives out' is the 'thingness' of things.

Briefly expressed, then, in its reduction of everything to pure resource, *Gestell* drives out, makes us 'oblivious' to, both the objectness and the thingness of beings. How, then, to reformulate the question as to how *Gestell* explains the violence of modern technological practice, does this double exclusion explain the violence of modernity? The answer seems to me the following.

16. Violence, violation or 'setting-upon' (QCT p. 27), is more than mere harm or damage. If I bump your car with mine thereby causing you whiplash, I harm but hardly violate you. What, then, is violation? How does it differ from mere harm? The difference, I suggest, is that violation is *essential* harm, harm to the 'essence' of something in Heidegger's sense of 'essence' in which it means *quidditas* or 'whatness' (ET p. 136). Violation is, in one way or another and to one degree or another, preventing something being (or becoming) what it is. A woman is violated when she finds herself forced to live not as a person but as a mere sex object – a mere sexual 'resource' – a forest, an intricately wrought

and finely balanced ecological system, is violated when its exploitation as timber no longer allows it to be the ecological system that it is.

Gestell, however, drives out our ability even to *see* the whatness, objectness, the in-itselfness of beings. By doing so it deprives us of the *ability* to stand in a gentle, care-ful as opposed to violent, relation to things. If one cannot see the forest as anything more than a supply of cellulose (QCT p. 18), the river as anything more than a power source, or the person as anything more than a sexual resource or productive unit, then the beings in question show up as available for, in Heidegger's words, the technological will's '*unconditional self-assertion*' (WPF p. 111; my emphasis). Since nothing shows up save their resource-ful being-for-us, nothing presences to 'condition', to act as a possible limit upon, their manipulation and exploitation as resource (apart from the requirements of their own efficient and sustained functioning as resource). As a hammer is not violated, not abused, by a hammering that takes it to its limits, so a river is not violated by its 'unconditional' use as a hydro-electric power source since that, from the perspective of *Gestell*, is all it is. *Gestell* makes violation inevitable because, fundamentally, it takes away the concept of violation.

By occluding the objectness of beings, *Gestell* takes away the *ability* to stand in a care-ful, non-violent relation to them. But by occluding *poiesis*, the thingness of beings, it takes away the *will* to stand in such a relationship. By occluding the sense of the world as 'brought forth', as the self-revelation of the divine, it destroys the sense of it as a sacred place – as, so to speak, the face of God – and, as such, a place to be reverenced and cared for. And by doing that it takes away the motivation to a gentle rather than violent technology.

Notice a certain peculiarity about the relation between *Gestell* and the violence of modern technology: it over-determines it. By obscuring the in-itselfness, the objectness of beings, it takes away the ability to care for them. But by taking away their thingness it takes away the will to do so. Both the ability and the will to care for things are, however, necessary to the coming into being of a non-violent technology.[14] Hence, by destroying the *two*

---

[14] It might be thought that this separation of ability and will is a mistake, that for things to show up as they are in themselves – for the forest, for example, to show up as the delicate, and finely balanced ecological system that it is – is sufficient to generate a care-ful relation to them. But this is a mistake. A timber-miller, for example, may, through the efforts of environmentalists and their allies in the media, be brought to the vivid and inescapable

necessary conditions of such a technology, *Gestell* makes the violence of modern technology *doubly* inevitable.

17. If the preceding discussion is sound, we now understand why it is that *Gestell*, the disclosure of everything as pure resource, is the 'essence' of modern technological practice, the explanatory ground of its unique violence. But Heidegger claims, too, it will be remembered, that 'metaphysics' is that ground. If, then, his philosophy is to constitute a genuine unity, if the philosophy of technology is to be shown to be, as he claims, grounded in the philosophy of B/being, we must answer the question as to how it is that when technology is thought in an 'essential' way, in other words, as *Gestell*, its meaning 'coincides with' that of 'completed metaphysics' (OM p. 75). Why is it, in other words, that the 'age of *Gestell*' is one and the same phenomenon as the 'age of metaphysics'?

The answer to this question, however, is relatively obvious. The age of *Gestell*, we saw, is the age in which the world is disclosed as *pure* resource. In the 1938 'Age of the World Picture' Heidegger expresses this idea by saying that modernity is the 'age of the world picture' not merely in the sense that we have a picture of the world – every age has that – but in the sense that we live in the age of the world *as* 'picture', the age in which the world, in the sense of 'that which is in its entirety' (AWP p. 129), has 'become picture' (AWP p. 130), has become *nothing but* our resource-ful picture of it. But if this is so, if modernity is the age in which man inhabits the 'delusion' that 'everywhere and always [he] encounters only himself' (QCT p. 27), if it is the age that takes its resource-ful picture of things to *exhaust* the totality of what there is, then it is the age of absolutization, the absolutization of its technological disclosure of B/being. Heidegger puts this by saying that *Gestell* 'disguises' (TT p. 36), i.e. misinterprets, its own status as a horizon of disclosure; it 'conceals revealing itself' (QCT p. 27). This is why it 'drives

knowledge that his 'unconditional' exploitation of a forest as a supply of timber is the destruction of a unique and irreplaceable ecological system. This, however, is not, by itself, sufficient to 'condition' his exploitative practice, for he simply may not *care* about irreplaceable ecologies, may care about them as little as the Japanese government seems to care about whales. One might, of course, persuade him to care by pointing out the 'conservation value' of the forest as a 'recreational resource'. But this will not persuade him to care for the forest in its 'ownness', in and for itself. To generate that kind of care – the only kind capable of generating a genuinely 'gentle' technology – only the forest's showing up as a *sacred* forest is sufficient.

out' (*ibid.*) the possibility of any disclosure of reality other than itself and becomes, therefore, metaphysics.

The festival

18. Before leaving the topic of *Gestell*, a final question. Why is it that the metaphysical misinterpretation of the technological disclosure of B/being – that which drives out both the objectness and the thingness of beings and so generates a violent technology – has achieved world-historical dominion for the first time in modernity? Why is the absolutizing of the technological disclosure of B/being, metaphysics, *unique* to modernity? Why are we so different from pre-modernity, from, paradigmatically, the Greeks? What did they have that we have lost? What, in other and better words (see section 7 above), do we need to acquire in order to overcome the violence of the age?

The human being, we have seen, is *essentially* a technological being. The disclosure of things as resource characterizes *every* culture, *every* epoch. Every age has its version of the technological disclosure of B/being. But Heidegger makes an even stronger claim: the disclosure of things as *pure* resource, the 'mak[ing] over' of the world for 'the unconditional self-assertion' of the technological 'will' is

the hidden nature of [not just modern but rather *all*] technology. Only in modern times [however] does this nature begin to unfold as a destiny of the truth of all beings as a whole; until now, its scattered appearances and attempts had remained incorporated within the embracing [*umfassenden*] structure of the realm of culture and civilization. (WPF pp. 111–12)

This passage says three things. First, that the *threat* of *Gestell* is inseparable from technology *as such*, is, that is, a threat, not just to modernity, but rather to *every* epoch. Heidegger emphasizes this point in commenting on Rilke's remark that in contrast to the authentic homes of our grandparents' time, modern houses 'intruding from America' are 'empty, indifferent things, sham things, *dummies of life*' (not houses but, as one might put it, 'accommodation resources'). Heidegger says: 'it is not that Americanism [i.e. *Gestell*] first surrounds us moderns with its menace; the menace of the . . . essence of technology surrounded even our forefathers and their things' (WPF p. 108).

The second point made in the above passage is that though *Gestell* has *threatened* every epoch it is only in modernity that the threat has become a reality. Only in modernity has *Gestell* become a 'destiny', become, that is, an *epoch-defining* disclosure, a disclosure of 'world-historical' significance.

The third point is that what, in pre-modern times, kept 'the danger' (QCT *passim*) threatened by all technology at bay was something lying within the 'embracing' structure of pre-modern culture. The reason, then, for the world-historical take-over by *Gestell* and by metaphysics is that we have lost something that pre-modern culture had, some antidote to the metaphysical misinterpretation of the technological disclosure of B/being. The question before us now, therefore, is: what is this antidote?

19. First, however, we need to ask: why is the reduction of things to pure resource a 'menace' implicit in *all* technological activity?

Schopenhauer observed not only that work requires things to show up in work-suitable, resource-ful ways but also that, from within the work-perspective, things tend to show up in *only* resource-ful ways. His explanation emphasizes the role of time, or of, rather, its lack:

> a mind that is vividly aroused by willing . . . is incapable of comprehending the purely objective nature [the being-in-itself] of things. For willing and its [technological] aims make it so one-sided, that it sees in things only what refers to these . . . For example, a traveler who is anxious and in a hurry, will see the Rhine and its banks only as a dash or stroke, and the bridge over it only as a line intersecting that stroke. In the head of a man filled with his own aims, the world appears just as a beautiful landscape does on the plan of a battlefield.[15]

Heidegger makes a similar point (without, however, acknowledging the extent to which he is simply repeating Schopenhauer, a philosopher to whose considerable virtues he is, sadly, entirely blind): when things are viewed from a practical point of view, viewed, that is, as 'equipment', their being-in-itself 'disappears into usefulness' (OWA p. 46). There is, therefore, a natural tendency inherent in *all* technological activity for things to be drained of their non-resource-ful properties, to become, as I earlier put it, etiolated. In *Being and Time* Heidegger ontologizes this by insisting that the way beings show up in the (any) life-world is as 'ready-to-hand' (resource), and that their 'present-at-handness' (being-in-itself) shows up at all only in those exceptional

---

[15] *The World as Will and Representation*, 2 vols., trans. E. F. J. Payne (New York: Dover, 1969) vol. II p. 381.

situations where there is a breakdown in the smooth functioning of technological activity.

Work, in Heidegger's 'broad and multifarious' sense, is, we have seen (in section 11 above), not just a, but rather *the* central feature of human existence. It is its 'average everydayness'. This means that the technological disclosure of B/being is the way the world shows up at its most 'familiar', most 'ordinary'. Heidegger says: 'when familiarity becomes boundless ... nothing is able to withstand technical mastery' (ET p. 147). In other words, unless something interrupts the everyday world of work, unless some 'displacement' occurs, unless something 'extraordinary [extra-ordinary] ... thrust[s] down' the 'long-familiar', unless something 'transport[s] us out of the realm of the ordinary' in such a way as to 'transform our accustomed ties to the world ... all our usual doing and prizing, knowing and looking' (OWA p. 66), then 'technical mastery' becomes 'boundless'; i.e. 'unconditional' (WPF p. 111). Unless, in other words, something extra-ordinary happens the world shows up as pure resource. Unless the human being 'from time to time gets taken [out of the ordinary and] up into [its] ... originary essence' (ET p. 151), the technological disclosure of B/being becomes absolutized and metaphysics has arrived.

But – here we come to the observation that only in modernity has *Gestell* become a 'destiny', achieved a world-historical take-over – the Greeks did *not* succumb to the violence of metaphysics. Something indeed happened to 'thrust down' the 'long-familiar' and 'transport' them into the extra-ordinary. Unlike us, the Greeks had an antidote to metaphysics, an antidote we, to our great misfortune, have lost. What, then, to repeat, is this antidote?

20. In 'The Origin of the Work of Art' Heidegger calls it 'the artwork'. In the discussions of Hölderlin's 'Remembrance [*Andenken*]' (GA 52 and GA 4 pp. 79–151) he calls it 'the holiday' or – the most illuminating of the three descriptions – 'the festival'.

What, asks Heidegger, is the holiday; the *authentic* holiday, that is, the holy-day? First of all, obviously, it is a 'setting oneself outside of everyday activity, the cessation of work' (GA 52 p. 64), a 'break from work [*Arbeitspause*]' (GA 4 p. 102). As such it is a stepping out of 'the usual', the 'everyday ... [in which] things stand to us in the perspective of usefulness ... and at the same time not in their essences' (GA 52 p. 65).

This 'stepping out' is (for reasons we do not yet understand) the antidote to *Gestell*. We in modernity, however, have lost it. We have lost the authentic holiday. There is, to be sure, something we *call* the holiday and regard as a 'break from work'. But really, this is nothing but 'rest and recreation [*Mittel der Entspannung und Erholung*]' and, as such, 'work-serving'. Speaking of our culture as a whole, we can say that since, as an institution, the holiday has become just a form of stress-relief (like nearly all modern art, according to Heidegger[16]) the point of which is to preserve our efficiency as workers, the modern holiday is 'defined in relation to work' (GA 52 p, 64).

The authentic, the Greek, holiday is first of all, then, *genuine* 'time out', a *genuine* work-pause, a stepping out of the everydayness in which things show up as pure resource. Into what?

21. The most obvious reference for 'the festival' is the celebratory occasion in temple, amphitheatre, or Olympic stadium (OWA p. 43) which occurred 'from time to time' (ET p. 151) and during which the Greeks were (at least often) 'transported' (OWA p. 66) into the 'extraordinary'. That is what we might call the 'ontic' festival (or artwork). It is clear, however, that what really interests Heidegger is the 'ontological' festival, in other words that ecstatic state – ecstatic in both the ordinary sense and in the literal sense of 'standing out from'[17] the ordinary – in which everyday experience of the world is transformed into something quite different. While this is, perhaps, most likely to occur during the ontic festival it is not confined to such occasions. Heidegger identifies two features as constitutive of the festive state.

The first lies, he says, in the fact that time that is genuinely 'time out' from the harried world of everyday activity is a time of 'coming to oneself' (GA 4 p. 102): coming to oneself not in the sense of self-indulgence, of attending to pleasures one has denied oneself during work-time, but in the sense, rather, of 'coming to one's senses', escaping the perceptual 'illusions' (QCT p. 27) of harried everydayness. (Using Erik Fromm's language we might say that it is time for 'being' – for being oneself in a world that is itself – as opposed to 'having' (i.e. 'producing' in order to 'have').) The result is that things

---

[16] And Nietzsche according to whom modern art (especially Wagner's) is art for the 'work-weary'.

[17] From the Greek *ekstasis* and Latin *exstare*. Heidegger often employs 'ecstasy' is this way – and alludes to this meaning in his frequent writing of '*Existenz*' as '*Ek-sistenz*' (see, for example, LH pp. 247 ff.).

show up in their 'ownnesses' or 'essences' (GA 52 p. 65). We step out of the 'inauthenticity' (*Uneigentlichkeit* – un-ownness) of average everydayness and into 'the authentic that is always the inhabitual'[18] (*ibid.*).

'The inhabitual', Heidegger continues,

means here not the exotic, the sensational, the never-before-seen but rather the opposite: the inhabitual is the permanently essential, simple, and ownness of beings. (GA 52 p. 66)

In other words, in the festive mode of disclosure, things step out of the etiolation of everydayness and show up, instead, in their being-in-themselves (one might also say 'being-for-themselves', their 'own' being). Things show up, that is, as 'objects', show up in their 'autonomy' (see section 14 above).

The second defining feature of the festive state is that, in it, beings step out of 'the dull [*glanzlos*] overcastness of the everyday' (GA 4 p. 103) and into 'the radiance' (GA 52 p. 66).

What Heidegger means by 'the radiance' is best expressed in the first stanza of one of the Hölderlin poems that meant the most to him, 'As when on Holiday':

> As when on holiday, to view the fields
> Forth goes a farmer, at break of day,
> When all through the sultry night cooling flashes
> Have fallen and the thunder still rumbles afar
> And back into its channel the stream retreats
> And newly grows the grass,
> And heaven's gladdening showers
> Drip from the vine, and gleaming
> In peaceful sunlight stands the grove of trees:

('So', the second stanza begins – making it clear that the first two stanzas together constitute an extended simile – 'they', the poets, 'stand under propitious weather' (quoted by Heidegger at GA 4 p. 49). Poets, then, are those who are, *qua* poets, *permanently* 'on holiday', in the festive state.) In the discussions of Hölderlin's 'Remembrance' Heidegger explains the radiance in a way that is both more metaphysical (in the usual rather than Heidegger's

---

[18] 'Inhabitual' is Mcneill and Davis' illuminating rendition of 'das *Ungewöhnliche*' (the unusual or extraordinary) in their fine *Ister* translation. It allows one to see that the ontological festival does not always *have* to be time out from work as such, merely from habitual work. This point will shortly become clearer.

pejorative sense of the word) and more overtly subject-related than this. On
the ecstatic occasion we

step into the... intimation of the wonder that around us a world worlds, that there is
something rather than nothing, that there are things and we ourselves are in their midst.
(GA 52 p. 64)

We step, in other words, into the sense of the world as *poiesis*, as something
given to us, given not in the sense in which the given is a terminus to thought
and experience, but in the sense, rather, in which it is something 'granted' to us
in the self-disclosure of the divine and self-concealing Origin. Experienced as
such, one understands the world as something, contingent, fragile, precious,
something which, far from being *of course* there, *might not have existed at all*.
Subjectively this produces a profound sense of 'wonder' and 'gratitude' (WCT
pp. 139ff., GA 52 p. 197). Wonder that there is something rather than nothing,
gratitude because, whatever its darknesses (Hölderlin's distant 'rumbles' of
thunder), the world is still, for those with eyes to see, an extraordinarily
beautiful place: not just 'granted' to us, therefore, but rather 'gifted', gifted
by an extraordinary 'graciousness' (GA 10 pp. 309–10). It is this mood,
or mode, of disclosure – one of Heidegger's insights is that moods are not
inner feelings but rather ways beings as a whole are disclosed (GA 39 p. 82,
p. 89) – which makes the festive state *festive*. For festivals are, by definition
celebrations, celebrations of the world and our life in it, of the fact 'that there
are things and we ourselves are in their midst'.

22. Together, the two defining features of the festive mode/mood of
disclosure[19] have a profoundly transformative effect on action. Because beings stand in the numinousness of *poiesis* they emerge from the 'injurious

---

[19] Are the two features independent or connected features? Could one occur without the other?
The answer seems to me the following. Beings can, sometimes, show up in their 'objectness'
without showing up in their, in Heidegger's especially elevated sense, 'thingness'. Boredom or
depression, for example, it seems to me, clearly takes us out of 'the perspective of usefulness'
and allows beings to show up in their ownness. In idly watching the raindrop running down the
window pane the bored child may well be hypersensitive to the qualities that are its 'ownness'.
Yet there is no radiance to beings, rather, quite the opposite. The situations of equipmental
breakdown discussed in *Being and Time* – the car will not start and so, for the first time, we are
aware of its 'present-at-handness' – constitute another range of examples of objectness without
thingness. On the other hand, if beings show up in the 'wonder' of their thingness then, since
wonder necessarily abolishes the etiolating veil of everydayness, they must show up in their
objectness too.

neglect' (TT p. 45) they have suffered in the perspective of 'everydayness', begin to 'thing', to stand forth as the 'things' (in Heidegger's specially elevated use of the word) that they are. (Recall, from section 15 above, that the festive 'worlding of world' is equivalent to the 'thinging of the thing'.) As such, as radiant, holy beings, they show forth as beings to be reverenced and cared for. *Only* such radiance, such charisma, as we have seen, can move us to reverence and care for things. As Schelling saw, Heidegger observes, caring for things 'demands immanence in God, pantheism'.[20]

Poiesis, then, *moves*, motivates us to care for things. But the other feature of the festive state – that things show up in their being-in-themselves – is equally essential. Authentic care for things, as we have seen, is possible only if they show up in their 'ownnesses'.

Heidegger says that in the festive state, beings 'come to stand within the measure (*Mass*) of their essences', their whatnesses, and so, together with the 'lighting and shining' of the essential (GA 52 p. 66), 'demand of men that they observe this measure' (*ibid.*). Our 'care' for things ceases to be the pointless 'wearisomeness' of manipulating and exploiting beings for merely productive ends and becomes instead, 'obedience to a protecting' derived from an ecstatic 'belonging to the essential in all beings' (GA 52 p. 65).

23. Of course (as Matisse said, explaining his decision to abandon the Fauves) one cannot be in a state of ecstasy for ever. Though the work perspective and the festive perspective do not always have to be mutually exclusive – the woodturner who responds to the 'different shapes slumbering within the wood – to wood as it enters into man's dwelling with all the hidden riches of its nature' (WCT p. 14) may be *ecstatically at work* – they are, of necessity, usually so.[21] Nonetheless, the fact that the Greeks were 'from time to time

---

[20] *Schelling's Treatise on the Essence of Human Freedom* trans. J. Stambaugh (Athens: Ohio University Press, 1985) p. 85. Schelling actually says that 'freedom', being one's authentic self, demands pantheism. But, for reasons we will come to, Heidegger understands freedom – the 'positive' freedom of being true to one's 'real' self, not the merely 'negative' freedom of absence of external constraint on one's actions (ET p. 145) – as caring for things, 'letting them be' the beings they are (ET p. 144).

[21] Schopenhauer, it will be recalled, suggests that this has to do with lack of time. But work – traditional handwork, for example – does not have to be *frenetic* work. That work as such has to be, most of the time, unecstatic has, I think, to do with the necessity of technique and its inevitably routine, repetitive character. Work demands the habitual and so cannot – save for rare, but crucial, 'peak experiences' (as artists sometimes call the festive state) – be performed out of 'the inhabitual'.

taken into the originary essence of truth' (ET p. 151), the fact that they were, again and again (note the emphasis on *regularity* of worship common to all religions), taken into the festive state, profoundly modified the policies governing their work-practices.

To sum up. Though, as 'The Question concerning Technology' calls it, 'the extreme danger' (QCT p. 28) that is *Gestell*, i.e. metaphysics, threatened the Greeks as it threatens all humanity, they were saved from its world-historical take-over by 'the festival'. Since they inhabited the festive as well as the 'everyday' disclosure of reality, their 'being-in-the-world', that is to say (BT 239), their mode of *acting* in the world, was not determined by *Gestell*.

Modernity, however, has lost the authentic holiday. On the 'break from work' we are, generally, still 'at work'. We have become a culture of 'workaholics' – Ernst Júnger's observation, which profoundly impressed Heidegger (see QB *passim*), that the '*Gestalt* of the worker' has 'totalized' itself, has become the 'only game in town'. Nothing exists for us as an antidote to the 'danger' of *Gestell* which is the reason that what merely 'menaced' earlier epochs is becoming with us, ever more decisively, a reality. It is *Gestell* which determines our experience of both ourselves and our world, and hence our being-in that world.

This – the real importance, to repeat, of Heidegger's philosophy of technology, given the uncertain reality of his 'Greeks' – provides an important pointer to the character of 'the turning', whether it be the turning of our culture as a whole to a new, post-modern, age, or the personal turning made by you and me as individuals. If we are to overcome the violence of the modern technological relationship to reality we must learn, once again, how to inhabit the festive state, learn, in Fromm's language, to inhabit the state 'being' rather than that of 'having'. In Hölderlin's language, we must learn to become 'poets'.

4   Dwelling

1. In chaper 2 I identified three phenomena – the loss of the gods, the violence of technology, and homelessness, the loss of dwelling – as, for Heidegger, the principle symptoms of modernity's 'sickness [*Unheil*]', its 'destitution'. The underlying cause of each, we saw Heidegger to claim, is 'metaphysics'.

Why metaphysics should be the underlying ground of loss of the gods is, we saw in chapter 2, relatively obvious. And in the last chapter we saw why it is that metaphysics – the metaphysical interpretation of the technological disclosure of B/being, in other words, *Gestell* – underlies the violence of modern technological practice. It is now time to turn to the third symptom, homelessness. What, we need to ask, is this 'dwelling' we are said to have lost, and why should metaphysics be its fundamental cause?

What is dwelling?

2. 'To be a human being', says Heidegger, 'means . . . to dwell' (BDT p. 147). When I think the word 'man' properly, I think of 'a being who exists in a human manner – that is, who dwells' (BDT p. 156). That this is so is intimated by the fact that the '*bin*' of '*ich bin* (I am)' – the distinctively human form of the verb 'to be' – comes from the Old High German and Old English '*buan*', which means 'to dwell' (BDT p. 147). Dwelling is, for Heidegger, therefore, the human 'essence' (QCT p. 28, LH p. 257, PMD *passim*), 'essence', here, in the sense of *quidditas* or whatness (ET p. 136). The human essence is to be in the world as in a *Heimat* (homeland) or dwelling-place.[1] What is it for one's being-in-the-world to have this character?

Heidegger's answer is that to dwell is

to be at peace, to be brought to peace, to remain in peace. The word for peace, *Friede*, means the free, *das Frye* [in old German], and *fry* means: preserved from harm and

---

[1] This presents an obvious problem. How can modern man be 'homeless' if 'man's' essence is to dwell? I shall address this in section 9 below.

danger, preserved from something, that is, taken-care-of [*geschont*]. To free really means to care-for [*schonen*]. The caring-for itself consists not only in the fact that we do no harm to that which is cared-for. Real caring-for is something *positive* and happens when we leave something beforehand in its nature [*Wesen*], [or] when we gather [*bergen*] something back into its nature, when we 'free' it in the real sense of the word into a preserve of peace. To dwell, to be set at peace, means to remain at peace within the free sphere that cares-for each thing in its own nature. *The fundamental character of dwelling is this caring-for.*[2] (BDT p. 149)

The point to notice here about this rich and subtle piece of writing is the (surely intentional) slide from the dweller taken as the *object* of caring-for, to the dweller as its *subject*. The passage begins, that is, by telling us that to dwell is to be safe, secure, free of care, to be *taken-care-of*, but ends by telling us that to dwell is to be one who *cares-for* things – the things, clearly, that belong to the dwelling-place. To notice this slide[3] is to see that Heidegger explicates dwelling in terms of, not one, but rather two fundamental conditions. To dwell is (a) to be cared-for in the dwelling-place and (b) to care for the things of the dwelling-place. Both of these conditions, I suggest, correspond to intuitive notions about being-at-home (or, as I shall sometimes say, modifying the word to capture the sense of the German *heimisch*, being 'homely'). To dwell is to experience oneself as safe in, cared-for by, the dwelling-place in a way one is not safe in or cared-for by the foreign, and to dwell is to care for the place where one dwells in a way one does not care for the place where one does not. People do not litter their homes (if homes they have) in the way they litter motorways. I shall discuss these conditions in turn.

Death

3. To dwell, to repeat, is to be in, as the old German word has it, *das Frye*, a 'free' place in the sense of a place where one is 'preserved from harm and danger'. To dwell is to experience oneself as, in spite of the risks and dangers which confront all human beings wherever they are, in some ultimate sense, *secure*. Secure from what?

---

[2] I prefer my 'caring-for' to Hofstadter's 'sparing and preserving', firstly, because it corresponds to the fact that Heidegger uses one word, *Schonen*, rather than two, but secondly and more importantly, because 'sparing and preserving' fails to capture the creative, 'freeing' aspect (in other words, *techne*) which Heidegger (as we will see in much greater detail in chapters 7 and 8) takes to be an essential aspect of *Schonen*.

[3] The slide has completed itself with the appearance of 'we' in the fourth sentence of the passage. The third sentence is transitional.

The ultimate threat to one's security is, of course, death; death understood as annihilation, nothingness. So if one experiences oneself as ultimately – 'ontologically', as one might put it – secure, then one experiences oneself as secure even in the face of death. One confronts death, that is, not with fear but rather with – to use a favourite word of Heidegger – *Gelassenheit*, equanimity (DT *passim*[4]): 'mortals dwell in that they initiate [*geleiten*] their own nature – their being capable of death as death – into the use and practice of this capacity, so that there may be a good death', a death faced with equanimity. Such an initiation, Heidegger continues, is by no means a coming-to-terms with annihilation but is, rather, an overcoming of the thought that death, the terminus or 'goal' of life, is an 'empty nothing' (BDT p. 151).

In 'What are Poets for?', appropriating Rilke's language and thought, Heidegger describes the life of modern humanity as a 'constant negation of death' (WPF p. 125). Since the fundamental term *Being and Time* uses to picture 'average everyday', 'inauthentic' Dasein's stance to death is *evasion*, 'negation' means here, I suggest, 'evasion'. Most of us are unable to look death directly in the face without terror: terror before the 'abyss' (*Abgrund*, absence of ground) (WPF p. 92), the 'empty nothing' (BDT p. 151), horror at the void. Nearly always, therefore – reasonably enough, one might think – we avoid such confrontations. We do this by deploying an ingenious variety of evasive strategies. For example, we avoid using the word 'death', preferring to talk of putting beloved pets 'to sleep' and of ourselves as 'passing on'. (The Christian doctrine of personal immortality might itself, of course, be regarded as the ultimately 'inauthentic' evasion of death.) Unlike non-Western cultures we tuck not just the word but also the phenomenon of death out of sight. We conceal the aged in rest homes, the dying in hospitals, and their bodies in crematoria. Most of us have seen few, if any, dead bodies.

Another evasion of death is to treat it as an accidental rather than essential feature of the human condition. We treat it as a 'failure of the health system'

---

[4] The translation of *Gelassenheit* as 'releasement' in the 'Discourse on Thinking' responds to the fact that, in Heidegger's rich and idiosyncratic use of the word, it means, centrally, releasement from *Gestell* and (an echo of Heidegger's early training in phenomenology) 'to the things' (DT pp. 54–5). To enter the state of *Gelassenheit* is, in other words, for things to rise out of their 'injurious neglect' (TT p. 45), for them to appear *as* the 'things' they are, for them to 'thing'. It is, in short, to enter the festive state, to experience the *Ereignis*. None of this, however, should be allowed to obscure the fact that the ordinary meaning of 'equanimity' is *part* of what Heidegger means by *Gelassenheit*. See, for example, the first stanza of Heidegger's poem 'Cézanne' quoted and discussed in HPA chapter 4 section 19.

for which someone, of course, has to be to blame.[5] Or we treat it as a joke, with nervous, Woody Allenish humour. ('I'm not afraid of death – I'd just rather not be there when it happens', while satirizing evasion of death, is itself an evasion, and hence – as Woody Allen, of course, is perfectly well aware – a self-satire.)

In section 53 of *Being and Time* Heidegger identifies a more profound and subtle evasion. Typically, he points out, while paying lip-service to the fact that we will certainly die 'some time' we refuse to acknowledge that death may happen *at any moment*.[6] By this device, by telling ourselves 'Of course, I'll die sometime – but certainly not today', and by saying this every time the thought of dying arises, we effectively provide ourselves with a 'guarantee' of immortality. Death, while it certainly will happen to Young, happens to a *future* Young, one to whom I, the *present* Young, bear only the most distant relationship, if indeed any relationship at all.[7]

In 'What are Poets for?' Heidegger makes an interesting connexion between evasion of death and life in *Gestell*: 'the [unconditional] self-assertion of technological objectification is the constant negation of death' (WPF p. 125). Obviously *Gestell* cannot evade death. Since only individuals die, Heidegger

---

[5] In the mid-1990s there occurred, on New Zealand television, a pre-election debate between party leaders on the topic of health. The members of the live audience were given electronic devices which enabled them to respond with varying degrees of favour or disfavour to what the participants were saying as they were saying it. The cumulative result was displayed as a kind of constantly fluctuating graph-line at the bottom of the screen which was known as 'the worm'. At one point, the incumbent Prime Minister, Jim Bolger (a Catholic), exasperated at constant carping over the failures of the health system, expostulated: 'Of course, death will always be associated with the health service.' The worm hit an all-time low and Bolger went on to lose his parliamentary majority.

[6] In the Middle Ages many churches had a figure of St Christopher at the entrance. By touching it as one entered one guaranteed that one would not die suddenly (i.e. without being able to confess one's sins) *today*. Up until quite late in the nineteenth century statistics were such that for all the years between the ages of about twenty and seventy one was as likely to die in any one year as any other. Unlike us, in other words, pre-modern man had no statistical warrant for supposing that death would first concern him in his seventies or eighties. Facts such as these suggest that *Being and Time* was wrong to suggest that evasion of the at-any-momentness of death is, to a constant degree, a universal human disposition and that later Heidegger is right to regard evasion of death as a phenomenon especially characteristic of the modern West.

[7] Evasion of death is a theme common to both *Being and Time* and to later Heidegger. Later Heidegger's account, however, of what it is that constitutes the proper overcoming of such evasion is profoundly different from that of earlier Heidegger. On what one might call the 'reversal' in Heidegger's treatment of death and its centrality to 'the turning' in general, see footnote 10 below, HPA chapter 4 sections 7–8, and my 'What is Dwelling? The Homelessness of Modernity and the Worlding of World' in *Heidegger, Authenticity, and Modernity: Essays in Honor of Hubert L. Dreyfus* (Cambridge.: MIT Press, 2000), vol I, pp. 187–203.

must have in mind, here, individuals who live within *Gestell* – individuals who are, as we might put it, thoroughly 'gestelled' – as the death-evaders *par excellence*.

The thought, here, I suggest, examines the question as to why it is that the modern human being, quite typically, is perfectly prepared to regard not only others but also *himself* as a mere 'human resource', as a mere cog in the global mechanism of consumption and production, or, better put, a mere information processor, a junction-box within the cybernetic network.

The important thing about information processors is that their consciousness is entirely *outwardly* directed, directed to the task at hand. Consciousness of mortality is, however, self-directed, *inwardly* directed, consciousness. Hence, information processors do not have consciousness of mortality, can not fear death.[8] Abandoning metaphor, to become nothing but an obedient, efficient and reliable 'human resource', in other words a 'workaholic', is to have a purely outer consciousness and therefore to evade knowledge of mortality. The life of a pure 'human resource' thus presents itself as a kind of narcotic, an evasion of mortality. (Sartre makes, I think, a not unrelated point with his celebrated example of the robotic waiter who tries to make the role of being a waiter consume his entire being.) Submission to *Gestell* is, then, yet another technique for evading 'ownership' (WPF p. 96) of death.[9]

We expend, then, a tremendous amount of psychic energy, deploy a great variety of measures, to 'shield' (WPF p. 125) ourselves from death, to achieve ontological security. In the end, though, they are all, of course, futile. Though by evading a direct confrontation we evade the terror of death, the knowledge remains and our lives – as Kafka saw perhaps more clearly than anyone else – are riddled by anxiety, the inevitable result of repressing, rather than conquering, terror. Anxiety is, of course, inconsistent with security. It follows, therefore, that evasion is a mistaken strategy for achieving ontological security. Some different strategy must be found, one which, by overcoming

---

[8] It is possible to speculate on the extent to which the currently fashionable programme of showing the mind to be a computer is motivated by fear of death.

[9] Heidegger seems to make something very close to this point in 'Overcoming Metaphysics'. Since for modern man beings are 'suspended' in a 'complete emptiness', an emptiness which has to be 'filled up', i.e. obliterated, 'the only way to escape it is incessantly to arrange beings in the constant possibility of being ordered as the form of guaranteeing aimless activity' (OM pp. 86–7).

the thought of death as entry into an 'empty nothing', enables us to look it directly in the face, with equanimity, without terror.

4. Why is it that modern humanity experiences anxiety in the face of death, cannot, in Rilke's words, 'read the word "death" *without* negation' (WPF p. 125)? For Heidegger, of course, the reason is metaphysics, oblivion of Being. Absolutizing our horizon of disclosure and so misconstruing our world of beings as constituting the totality of what there is, locked into the two-dimensionality of taking the 'globe of Being' to be a flat, illuminated disk, we take its other 'side' to be an *absolute* – an, as Heidegger puts it, 'empty', a completely 'privative-negative' (GA 15 p. 363) – 'nothing'. In place of an *Urgrund* (WPF p. 101) on which we might found our being we confront only an 'abyss [*Abgrund*]' (WPF p. 92). Gripped by metaphysics, in other words, we take it that there is *no* other 'side' to our world of beings, that its inhabitants are 'suspended' in 'a complete emptiness' (OM p. 86). Given such a taking, death presents itself, of course, as absolute annihilation. As a result, to avoid the terror of 'blindly staring towards the end' (BDT p. 151), life becomes the anxiety of evasion. But such a life can never possess the absolute security which, Heidegger holds, is one of the two hallmarks of dwelling.[10]

5. Since metaphysics is the source of anxiety about death the overcoming of metaphysics is the key to overcoming that anxiety. One needs, in other words, to understand that though the other side of world is indeed the 'nothing', nothing knowable or comprehensible by us – in other words, 'the mystery' – it is not the 'empty' or 'abysmal' nothing but rather the concealed side of the 'globe of Being', something which, though unknown, is nonetheless 'positive (the *positum*)' (WPF p. 124). One needs to understand, says Heidegger, borrowing Rilke's words, that 'death is the *side of life* that is averted from us, unilluminated by us', that 'death and the realm of the dead belong to the whole of beings as its other side', and that 'there are regions and places which, being averted from us, seem to be something negative, but are nothing of the kind if

---

[10] According to *Being and Time* both 'anxiety' and '*Un-heimlichkeit*' (BT p. 188), homelessness, are 'existential', structural features of human existence. And it is also the case that beyond the manifest world is '*das Nichts*', understood as the *absolute* nothing (BT 152). This misunderstanding of 'the nothing', which leads to the conclusion that dwelling is impossible, is the proof of the correctness of later Heidegger's assertion that 'metaphysics . . . is still dominant' (LH p. 256) in *Being and Time*. See, further, the references given in footnote 7 above.

we think all things as being within the widest orbit of beings' (WPF p. 125).
One needs to understand, in short, that as the 'shrine of the nothing . . . death
harbours within itself', not the abyss of annihilation, but rather 'the mystery
of Being itself' (T pp. 178–9).

Why exactly, however, should overcoming metaphysics, understanding 'the
nothing' to be, as we might put it, not the *ontological* nothing of the abyss
but rather the *epistemological* (as we might put it, the capital 'N') Nothing of
'the mystery of Being itself', be the overcoming of the terror of death? Why
exactly should grasping that, though 'ungraspable' (I p. 136) in literal (non-
poetic) thought, there is *something* – '*etwas ganz und gar Anderes* [something
completely and utterly Other]' (GA 15 p. 363) – beyond beings enable me
to face death with equanimity? One thing, to be sure, is obvious; that the
Other of beings must be exempt from the dissolution of beings, in particular
from that dissolution which is the death of the being I call myself. But why
should the knowledge that it survives my death be any more comforting than
the knowledge that, for example, the matter in my body does?

Clearly, if openness to the Other of beings is to enable me to face death
with equanimity that Other must be experienced as being, in some sense, *me*.
Heidegger points towards this direction of thinking by means of a distinction between the 'ego' and the 'self' that runs through the Hölderlin discussion of the 1930s and 40s (see, for example, GA 39 p. 68, pp. 86–8, GA 4
p. 102, p. 129, GA 52 p. 176). What we need to discover, put in terms of this
distinction, is that though, of course, the ego dissolves along with the body,[11]
something I regard as more authentically my 'self' (my 'real self', in Kantian
language) is unaffected by such dissolution. Why, then, should I regard the
Other of beings as constituting my authentic 'self'?

Let us recall what it is to overcome metaphysics. It is to enter, as I called
it, the 'festive state', the state in which the world shows up as the 'radiant',
holy place that it is, as Being's *poiesis*, the self-disclosure of the infinitely
self-concealing divinity, as a consequence of which (see chapter 3 footnote
19) beings show up in their 'ownness', show up as they are in themselves. The

---

[11] P. F. Strawson showed many years ago that the idea of disembodied survival of an ego makes
no sense. Briefly put, Strawson argues (following Kant) that human conscious is essentially
self-consciousness and that self-consciousness is consciousness of a point of view that persists
through time. The possibility, however, of such an enduring point of view, he suggests, required
identification with a body that is one among many bodies situated in space and persisting through
time. (See *Individuals* (London: Methuen, 1959).)

result is that instead of being the exploitation and violation of things that is the character of life in *Gestell*, our 'care' becomes 'obedience to a protecting' derived from an ecstatic 'belonging to the essential in all beings' (see chapter 3 section 22).

As Heidegger reads it, it seems to me, the untitled poem by Rilke that is the main focus of 'What are Poets for?' (quoted at WPF p. 99), in its own way, makes these same points. Rilke calls the order of things, the world-disclosure, in which we find ourselves 'the venture', a venture which is ventured forth by what he variously calls 'the *Urgrund*', 'nature', 'life', 'the un-heard of centre'. This ground or origin 'ventures' beings forth – beings that include, conspicuously, ourselves – 'flings' us into being. But it does not abandon us. For at the same time, whether we know it or not, it holds us in 'the pure draft', a 'gravitational pull' towards itself as the ever-withdrawing 'centre' (PLT pp. 101–6).[12]

If we are open to the 'draft' (*Bezug* – pull not push) then, as the poem puts it, 'we go *with* th[e] venture, will it' (WPF p. 99). Instead of exploiting and violating things for the purposes of purposeless production our concern becomes the preservation and completion of the order of things revealed to us in the festive state. Instead of standing to beings in the 'antithetical' relation of 'setting upon' (QCT p. 27) imposed on us by *Gestell*, we go '*with*' the venture, will *it*. Though we 'accomplish' much, we 'manufacture nothing' (WPF p. 120). Our care becomes not the cycle of production and consumption but rather, to repeat, 'obedience to a protecting' and completing derived from an ecstatic 'belonging to the essential in all beings'.

What has this to do with facing death without 'negation'? What has it to do with discovering a 'self' that is different from the mortal 'ego'?

Who you are, one might suggest, is determined by what you identify with. Identity is a function of identification. Moreover, what you identify with is what you care about. If I care for nothing but satisfying the desires of this ego then that is where my identification and hence my identity

---

[12] Heidegger was often critical of Rilke. Even in 'What are Poets for?', a talk given to honour the twentieth anniversary of Rilke's death, he observes that Rilke's language is the language of 'metaphysics'. But that there is an identity of thinking with respect to the 'pull' of the 'un-heard of centre' is put beyond doubt by the passage from 'What is called Thinking?' quoted in chapter 1 (section 8) where, speaking entirely in his own voice, Heidegger speaks of Being as that which, though it 'withdraws' from us, 'draws us along by its very withdrawal' catches us, like 'migratory birds', in its 'pull'.

lies. But if I care for my family more than my individuality then my primary identification lies with it. Again, if I am prepared to sacrifice my life out of love for my country then my primary identification, my primary self, at least during the time of this preparedness, is my country. If, then, what I most of all care about is the world-'centre''s venture then it is with it that my primary identification lies. In other words, not the ego but rather the world-centre itself constitutes my primary 'self'. Overcoming metaphysics entails a relocation of the 'I'. It is this self-transcendence, I think, that Heidegger refers to when he calls the experience of the *Ereignis* as an experience of *'transport [Entrückung]* and enchantment' (GA 65 p. 70; my emphasis).

Rilke makes the relevance to death of this ecstatic self-transcendence explicit in the following passage. True security, he says, lies 'outside all protection'. It is to be found not in evasion of death (only someone locked into metaphysics and hence into identification of the self with the ego has an even *prima facie* need to evade death) but rather where 'life'

. . . creates for us a safety – just there where the pure forces' gravity rules. (WPF p. 99)

The thought here, it seems to me, is that what makes us truly 'safe' in the face of death is standing in 'draft' of the 'gravitational pull' which, as it were, draws us upwards and into the 'centre'. The same thought, I think, is expressed by Hölderlin in the introduction to *Hyperion*, where he identifies 'the peace of all peace . . . the goal of all our striving, whether we understand it or not' as 'unification of ourselves with nature, with the One infinite totality' (quoted by Heidegger at GA 52 p. 176). And by Hermann Hesse in the poem which Richard Strauss set to music as the third of the 'Four Last Songs' (Strauss' final preparation for death):

> And the spirit unguarded
> longs to soar on free wings
> so that, in the magic circle of the night,
> it may live deeply and a thousandfold.

Rilke's 'un-heard of centre' is, of course, the 'plenitude' of Heidegger's Being. In Heidegger's own language, therefore, equanimity in the face of death lies in unification with Being. (Hence, the 'self' which, in ecstatic moments, triumphs over the 'ego' is really the '*Self*'.) One cannot, however, experience that unification from within the cage of metaphysics. It follows, then, that genuine security lies – not in evasion of death – but in overcoming metaphysics, overcoming 'oblivion of Being'.

6. The second aspect of dwelling, we saw, consists in one's being, not the object but rather the subject of caring-for. It consists in being, not the violator, but rather the 'guardian' or 'shepherd of Being' (T p. 184, LH p. 252), of its self-disclosure as world. The dweller is one who 'lets beings be' (ET p. 144) in both the passive sense of 'sparing and preserving' and the active sense of *techne*, 'letting what is coming arrive'. Why, we need now to ask, is our failure of care, failure to live according to our 'essences', the consequence of metaphysics?

The answer to this question we have already seen, so we merely need to remind ourselves briefly of the contents of chapter 3 sections 13–23.

Heidegger asks himself what the conditions are under which dwelling as guardianship does and does not occur. It occurs, as we know, when beings show up in their radiant 'ownness', when the world shows up in charismatic 'authenticity [*Eigentlichkeit*]' (compare GA 52 p. 65). We care-for beings when, and only when, they show up as 'things' (and so, too, as 'objects'). Guardianship occurs if and only if beings show up 'from time to time' in the 'festive' or '*Ereignis*' experience.

When metaphysics sets in, however, beings become dimmed down to the single dimension of resource. They show up in neither their radiance nor ownness but rather as items available for 'unconditional' technological exploitation and violation – except, of course, that the idea of violation makes no sense.

In the life of 'metaphysical man', then, the authentic and 'enchanted' (GA 65 p. 70) world of things and objects is obscured. In its place 'semblance comes to power' (ET p. 146): all that shows up are the *ersatz* things of *Gestell*, Rilke's '*dummies of life*' (PLT p. 113). Instead of the 'guardian' of 'things' the human being becomes an exploiter of resources.

7. To sum up, therefore, dwelling, the human essence, is threatened by metaphysics, i.e. *Gestell*, in two fundamental ways. First, it deprives the human being of, as I have called it, 'ontological' security – knowledge of his membership of the realm that is beyond death – and hence of equanimity in the face of death. And second, it renders him incapable of caring-for things,

of dwelling as guardianship. In place of the serene guardian man becomes the anxious abuser.

The human essence

8. Heidegger's description of the life of dwelling is, no doubt, *attractive* and his description of the life of metaphysical man highly unattractive. Attractiveness, however, is not sufficient to establish a claim about the human *essence*. And neither are Heidegger's suggestive, but (since they are specific to the German language) hardly conclusive, remarks about the derivation of '*ich bin*' (I am) from '*buan*' (to dwell). The question presents itself, therefore, as to why we should accept the claim that 'when I say "a man" and in saying this word think of a being who exists in the human manner [I think of a being] . . . who dwells' (BDT p. 156).

To this question may be added another. An 'essence' in the above sense is something *every* being of a certain kind has and something that it has *all* of the time. It is that in virtue of which a being counts as a being of that kind. (Compare, for instance, the traditional 'man is a rational animal' to which 'man is the being who dwells' is clearly a deliberate challenge.) Yet modern man is, according to Heidegger's own description, the 'homeless' one: '*the* plight' of modernity is 'man's homelessness' (BDT p. 161). So, it seems, not all men dwell. How, then, one might well wonder, could dwelling possibly be the human essence?

9. The answer to the first question lies in Heidegger's philosophy of B/being and in the meditation just completed. We *do* all inhabit a holy world, we have seen, a world that is the self-disclosure of the self-concealing divinity. We all inhabit the 'immanence of God'. It follows that we all are, in fact, secure in the face of death, that our true 'Self' is not the frightened 'ego' but rather Being itself, the venturer of the whole 'venture' to which we belong. And it follows, too, since to inhabit a holy place is to inhabit a place that *ought to be* reverenced and cared-for, that we inhabit a world of which we are the 'guardians' – indeed the *sole* guardians – in the sense that it is our mission and task to care-for Being's 'venture'. This is the *truth* of the matter which is why, whether we know it or not, dwelling is our essence, and the world our homeland.

How, then, can it be maintained without contradiction that modern man is homeless? Heidegger moves to clarify this puzzling situation in the 'Letter on Humanism'. In the 'nearness of Being', he says, in, that is, 'the clearing of the *Da* [here], man dwells . . . without yet being able properly to experience and take over this dwelling' (LH p. 257).

That we all dwell – inhabit the 'nearness to Being', the 'immanence of God' – is, we have just seen, the truth of the matter. Dwelling is our essence, 'essential' dwelling, as we may call it, something we all possess. In modernity, however, we fail to understand our essential dwelling, fail to 'experience and take [it] over'. Encaged by metaphysics we fail to experience either our ultimate security or our mission of guardianship. That is why, though 'essentially' dwelling, modern humanity, in another sense – let us call it the 'existential' sense – fails to dwell. It fails to dwell because it fails to experience the 'nearness' of Being. '[Existential] homelessness is the symptom of oblivion of Being' (LH p. 258). The key, then, to seeing that there is, in fact, no contradiction between 'man dwells' and 'modern man is homeless' is to understand that Heidegger implicitly operates with two senses of 'dwelling': essential dwelling that is possessed by all human beings all of the time, and existential dwelling which consists in *understanding* one's essential dwelling and living in the light of that understanding.

5   The turning

1. In chapter 2, I distinguished three phases in Heidegger's medico-theological thinking about the 'sickness' of our culture: identification of symptoms, identification of their cause and, finally, the prescription of a therapy. Our study of the first two phases is now completed. The leading symptoms of modernity's spiritual sickness are: the flight of the gods, the violation of both human and non-human nature, and 'homelessness', modern man's loss of (existential) dwelling. And the underlying cause of each of these symptoms, the *fundamental* sickness of modernity, is 'metaphysics'.

So much for diagnosis, now for therapy. What, Heidegger asks, speaking, here, the language of theology rather than medicine, 'can save us' (S p. 107)? How, that is, are we to bring about 'the turning' (*Kehre*, closely related to *Bekehrung*, 'conversion')[1] to a post-metaphysical, post-*Gestell*, post-modern age?[2]

In order to understand what (if anything) we can do to bring it about we must ask, first, in what the turning consists.

The rejection of Luddism

2. The first thing Heidegger does in the important essay of 1949 called 'The Turning' is to dispose of Luddism. That the turning should happen (if it happens), he says, 'in no way means that technology, whose essence lies in *Gestell*, will be abolished [*beseitigt*]'. Technology will never be 'struck down' or 'destroyed' because its essence will never be 'overcome [*überwunden*]'. When the turn happens *Gestell* will not be overcome but rather, 'like grief or

---

[1] As already noted, Heidegger also uses 'the turning' to describe the transition in his own thinking that began in 1930. This gives us a powerful clue to the character of 'the turning' of our culture as a whole.

[2] To a *genuinely* post-modern age. Heidegger would regard our present so-called postmodernism as nothing more than 'consummation' of modernism (see N III p. 163), the completion of modernity's drive to reduce everything, including ourselves, to mere resource.

pain [*Schmerz*]' in human life, 'surmounted [*verwunden*] in a way that restores it to its yet concealed truth' (TT pp. 38–9). In the *Spiegel* interview he says that the 'technological world' will be not 'abolished' but, rather, 'assimilated and transformed [*aufgehoben*] in the Hegelian sense' (S p. 113).

The point, surely, about grief or pain is that its occasion, a loss or injury, remains long, or even for ever, after the pain has gone. (Pedantically speaking, time can *not* be relied upon to heal all wounds but only to take away their pain.) This suggests something initially surprising: though *Gestell* is the source of modernity's destitution, in the turn to a post-modern epoch 'it is not simply submerged and lost' (TT p. 37). Something of it remains even after the turn has completed itself. This is what might well seem surprising: since *Gestell* is the source of our destitution, one might expect 'salvation' to require its abolition, root and branch.

What we need to remind ourselves of, however, is that *Gestell* is not a simple but rather a complex, two-part phenomenon. As we saw in chapter 3, it is not just (a) the disclosure of everything as resource – that characterizes human 'everydayness' at *all* times and places – but rather (a) *together with* (b) the 'driv[ing] out [of] every other possibility or revealing', the disclosure of things as *nothing but* resource. *Gestell*, in other words, is (a) what I called 'the technological disclosure of B/being' *plus* (b) its metaphysical misinterpretation.

It is essential to recall that the *radix malorum*[3] in *Gestell* is revealed not by clause (a) but by clause (b). A technological disclosure of B/being is something possessed by every species of humanity, is the way things show up in every historical epoch nearly all of the time. Almost every moment of its waking life the human being as such is 'attuned' to things, 'comports' itself towards them, as resource.

There is, therefore, nothing wrong with the – with *any* – technological disclosure of B/being. It is an 'existential' of human life, the dominant feature of man's – not just degenerate man's – existence. What is wrong, rather, and, according to Heidegger, unique to modernity, is the metaphysical misinterpretation of that disclosure, a misinterpretation which excludes both the world's sacredness and its 'ownness'. What follows from this is that 'salvation' must consist, as 'The Turning' emphasizes, not in the abolition of our technological

---

[3] For Heidegger's occasional use of the language of 'evil' and the appropriateness of this piece of Chaucerian Latin see IM p. 46 and LH p. 267.

disclosure of B/being but in, rather, the abolition of its metaphysical misinterpretation.

Natural science

3. This, at any rate, represents Heidegger's thinking at its best. It has to be
said, however, that he himself is sometimes unclear, and, I think, confused, as
to where the *radix malorum* of modern technological practice is to be found.
The issue concerns natural science.

Like Schopenhauer and Nietzsche before him, Heidegger holds the interpretation of modern science as the 'disinterested' contemplation of the being-
in-itself of things to be naive (SR p. 167). Rather than being an alternative to
the technological disclosure of B/being modern science is essentially part of it.

What is characteristic of modern science is that it is completely (in the
most familiar sense of the word) 'mathematical'. As presented by fundamental physics – the science, as Heidegger notes, that is 'normative' for all of
modern science (AWP p. 118) – the world is made up of 'exact', completely
measurable, 'calculable', magnitudes. Why, asks Heidegger, should this be
so? Because the modern scientist has particularly sharp 'eyesight', a particularly penetrating insight into the heart of nature? Not at all. It is rather because,
prior to any empirical observations, science possesses a completely mathematical 'ground plan' in terms of which it decides, 'in advance' of empirical
research, nature must report her every move.

Why should science make this decision? Because, evidently, the more completely the world can be 'calculated' the more completely it can be predicted
and controlled. In short, far from being concerned to disclose the world in its
'ownness', science is just another disclosure of it in a 'work'-suitable way,
another disclosure of it as resource. Natural science, therefore, is not an alternative to the technological disclosure of B/being but a part of it. Like the
everyday disclosure of things as resource, it falls within 'the perspective of
usefulness'. It is our deepest look into the resourcefulness of things.

So far so good: modern science is part, not of the *bos theoretikos*, but rather
of the *bos praktikos* (SR p. 164). The problem, however, lies in a second claim
Heidegger often makes about modern science; as 'mathematical', it is *essentially* part of an assault upon, *necessarily* part of a programme to 'entrap the
real' in order to 'secure' it a way which Heidegger describes as 'dismaying'

(SR p. 168). Atomic physics, for example, is said to be, as such, an 'attack' upon life (WPF p. 112), and to have 'annihilated' the 'thing' by projecting it mathematically long before it annihilated it literally with the atom bomb (T p. 170). As mathematical, modern science *necessarily* shares in the violence of the modern technological enterprise in general. Pre-modern, Greek, science, on the other hand was not 'exact' (AWP p. 121) because it did not seek the control and exploitation of nature. It was part of the *bos theoretikos*, was a kind of disinterested phenomenology, 'the reverent paying heed to the unconcealment of what presences' (SR p. 164). Only a society gripped by metaphysics, dedicated to the violence of absolute control, the implication is, would have the impious temerity to, as it were, break things open and peer into their entrails.

4. There are at least three things seriously wrong with this line of thought. First, as Heidegger himself points out (AWP p. 118), '*ta mathematika*' originally meant, in Greek, that which man knows in advance of observation: not the 'numerical', in other words, but rather the '*a priori*'. What, however, is crucial to science as a technological activity is not the former but the latter sense. And in that sense, surely, *all* humanity has possessed science. Earliest humanity, for example, postulated, 'in advance of observation', a cosmos containing not only visible beings but also gods. And it postulated a complex set of laws connecting the moods of the gods with good and bad fortune and their good humour with various human practices such as worship and sacrifice. Though early man did not describe the structure of reality in numerical terms he practised science in the same sense as us and to the same end – to exert control over his environment.[4] The introduction of numerical quantification that made reality, for the first time, a measurable[5] phenomenon did not change the essential character of science: it just made it more effective. The idea of

---

[4] That humanity has always practised science in the sense of requiring nature to report herself in terms of an *a priori* 'ground plan' does not mean it has always *known* that to be the character of its science. The recognition of the importance of the *a priori* in science was an important advance in its philosophy which did not happen until the twentieth century. See, further, footnote 6 below.

[5] Heidegger dates the introduction of number into the fundamental vocabulary of science to the seventeenth century. The rendering of nature 'calculable' and the dawn of modernity happened together – in the age of Descartes. Modern research, however, has shown that the conceiving of reality in terms of numerical quantification had been proceeding apace since at least the thirteenth century. See A. W. Crosby, *The Measure of Reality* (Cambridge: Cambridge University Press, 1997).

an essential contrast between the character of modern and pre-modern science is, it seems to me, just a myth.

The second thing wrong with Heidegger's philosophy of science is that it is a betrayal of his own insight that there is nothing wrong with the technological disclosure of B/being – in *any* of its modes – as such. There is nothing wrong, that is, in seeking understanding and therefore a measure of control over reality. Though the ability to control can, of course, become abuse, as when it becomes control for the sake of 'unconditional' exploitation, it can also be the opposite. One cannot care-for a delicate ecological system unless one knows how it works and what the forces are that threaten to destroy it. The crucial point is that knowledge and the capacity for control that it brings are, in themselves, *neutral* phenomena. It is what we do with them that counts. Of course, if Heidegger is right (as he is) about the character of modernity in general, then modern natural science is, in fact, part of an enterprise of exploitation and violation. But that is due, not to the 'exact', the mathematical character of modern scientific knowledge as such, but rather to what, entrapped by metaphysics, we *do* with that knowledge. Heidegger's attack on modern science as such is a betrayal of his leading insight that the root of modernity's distress lies in neither its technological devices, nor the technological disclosure of B/being which makes them possible, but rather in metaphysics and the loss of the 'festival' that it entails.[6]

5. The third disastrous aspect of Heidegger's philosophy of science is that it is inconsistent with the anti-Luddism which, as we have seen, is a prominent and repeated theme in his later philosophy.

---

[6] One source of Heidegger's mistaken critique of the mathematical character of modern science lies in a tendency to confuse science with scientism (i.e. the metaphysical misinterpretation of science). In 'The Age of the World Picture', having explained that numerical quantification constitutes the *a priori* 'ground plan' of modern science, he goes on to say that, for science, 'only that which becomes object in this way *is* – is conceded to be in being . . . [the whole of the] being of beings is sought in such objectiveness' (AWP p. 127). In other words, Heidegger here claims, it is *part of* modern science to deny the being-in-itself of things, to deny that they have any being other than their being-for-science. That such scientism is, of necessity, the 'everyday' working attitude with which scientists do research I would not deny. Neither would I deny that many leading scientists, in reflective moments, too, are passionate and aggressive advocates of scientism. But that they all are is clearly false – both Newton and Einstein (the very greatest scientists in general, I would suggest) deny scientism – as is the claim that there is any *conceptual* connexion between science and scientism. That so *professional* (in the best sense of the word) a thinker as Heidegger should confuse the two is very surprising, and a sign, I think, of a certain lack of distance, of intellectual balance, concerning the topic of modern science.

In 1934, during the phase of his brief intoxication (though longer association) with Nazism, Heidegger was himself a Luddite. Holding, at that time, that the turning required the destruction of the world of modern technology and a return to the agrarian and hand-tool existence of pre-modern times, he called for the depopulation of the German cities and the resettlement of former industrial workers on to-be-conquered (Heidegger would have said reclaimed) land in Eastern Europe: the 'Pol Pot solution' to the problem of modern technology, as I have called it (HPN chapter 1 sections 14 and 21). Later Heidegger, however, abandons such obvious and unobvious idiocy. (Obvious idiocy (as well as wickedness) since a deindustrialized Germany would evidently not be able to defend its conquests against angry neighbours, armed with modern weapons and bent on regaining their land. Less obvious idiocy because, as will become clearer later on, since the turn is essentially an 'inner' affair, a matter of change of 'heart', no merely external or technological change can make it happen. The 'destitution' of metaphysics can, in principle, afflict a society that uses hand-tools just as easily and fully as it can afflict one that uses machine-tools.)

Later Heidegger understands, then, that after the turn we will remain in possession of modern machines. But that means that we must retain the scientific knowledge that makes their manufacture, operation, maintenance and refinement possible. Neither machines nor the science they presuppose will be 'abolished' by the turning. Rather, in a way we do not yet understand, they will play a transformed role in our lives (TT pp. 38–9, S p. 113, DT p. 54). Time and again Heidegger returns to this anti-Luddite theme: it is pointless to 'rebel helplessly against [technology] . . . and curse it as the work of the devil' (QCT p. 26); 'It would be foolish to attack technology blindly [and] . . . shortsighted to condemn it as the work of the devil' (DT p. 53); 'I am not *against* technology; have never [sic] spoken *against* technology nor against the so-called demonic elements in technology' (HIC p. 43); 'There is no demonry in technology' (QCT p. 28); and so on. If, then, there is no 'demonry' in modern technology neither can there be demonry in the disclosure of B/being by modern mathematical science which makes such technology possible.

6. Heidegger's philosophy of science is, then, something of a disaster since it is inconsistent with his philosophy of technology and renders his overall philosophy self-contradictory. On the one hand modern mathematical science

is *essentially* an assault on things, *necessarily* part of the violence of modern technology and is something, therefore, that has no place in a non-abusive society. Thought about this way, the turning has to be a Luddite revolution since to give up the knowledge on which they are based is to give up machines. Yet, for excellent reasons, later Heidegger insists that the turning cannot have that character, that it will take the form of a 'transformation' of the use, rather than 'abolition' of the phenomenon, of modern science and technology. Since this theme, as I shall attempt to show in the rest of the book, represents everything that is constructive, hopeful and truly important in Heidegger's later philosophy, his anti-sciencism should simply be abandoned as a curious legacy of the Luddism of the Nazi years.[7]

7. As already indicated, the non-Luddite quality of Heidegger's best thinking emerges clearly in his account of the turning. Since it is not the technological disclosure of being, in any of its forms, but rather its metaphysical misinterpretation that is the root of modernity's destitution, it is the latter, not the former, which disappears in the turning.[8] The technological disclosure of being, and with it, modern science, remains in place. The turning consists in its being 'restor[ed] into its yet concealed truth' (TT p. 39). What does this mean?

Heidegger says that when the turning happens, our current 'clearing', *Gestell*, 'suddenly clears itself and lights up' (TT p. 44). It becomes, as we may put it, transparent. We are able to look through the resourcefulness of beings to see them in the 'wonder' of their ownness. They stand forth festively as both 'things' and 'objects'. By 'clearing' itself, the clearing, like a Swiss lake, reveals its 'depth'. That hitherto 'concealed truth' – the thingness and objectness of beings – is restored to them.

In short, when the turning happens we will give up neither machines nor the science which makes them possible. The difference it will make is that

---

[7] This is not to say that there is *nothing* of value in Heidegger's philosophy of science. His anti-inductivist account of the importance of the *a priori* in science, publicly presented in the 1938 'The Age of the World Picture', antedates by a number of years the critique of inductivism (the view that science first makes careful observations on the basis of which it eventually formulates tentative laws) presented by Popper and Kuhn that is, by now, widely accepted.

[8] How, it might be asked, does Heidegger *know* that the turning will take this form? How does he know there will not be a nuclear catastrophe that will return us to the pre-modern life-forms which, in 1934, he had hoped to achieve by somewhat less catastrophic means? He, of course, does not know. The point is, rather, that the turning as he describes it is, first, a *possible* form that it might take and, second, the form of the turning for which we should work, hope and pray (compare TT p. 49).

we will use the former and practise the latter, no longer as denizens of the night-time (WPF p. 91) world of *Gestell*, but rather as dwellers in the radiant world of the *Ereignis*, of the festival. We will then comport ourselves towards the things of our world as beings who have escaped the cage of metaphysics, have been restored to 'the full breadth of the space proper to [their]. . . essence' (TT p. 39). As beings that have achieved 'releasement' from metaphysics and 'to the things' (DT p. 54), we will give up exploitation and abuse and re-enter our essences as B/being's 'guardians'.

This will, of course, entail dramatic changes in our technological practices. As things stand forth in their holy 'ownness' they will stand forth *in* the abuse and violation, the 'injurious neglect' (TT p. 45), they have suffered in the age of *Gestell*. The holy landscape will show up as ravaged by urban sprawl, the rain forest as raped by clear felling, human beings as violated by their reduction to productive units. Violence (echoes, here, of the book of Revelation) will give way to 'gentleness', abuse to care and conservation.

Heidegger's account of the turning, his account of the way of being-in-the-world that is based on 'insight into that which is' (TT p. 46) rather than the 'illusion' of metaphysics, is thus profoundly critical with respect to modern technological practice. For all that, however, to repeat once again the central point of this chapter, the modern 'technological world' will remain. The new age will not be a return to the technology of the cave. Rather, it will deploy the resources of modern science and technology in a new way, the character of which I shall explore in chapters 7 and 8.

6   Fatalism

1. Many people, lay as well as professional thinkers, share in something resembling Heidegger's disquiet concerning the present state of our culture. Many, that is, share the sense that something vital that we once, at least to some degree, possessed is disappearing with ever-increasing rapidity from contemporary life – whether this expresses itself as a lament for the loss of 'family values' or of 'communal values', as dismay at the effect of human beings on the biosphere or at the scope and direction of gene technology. Many, too, I think, would be sympathetic to Heidegger's account of the turning that we need to make, an account which, for all its sound and fury, is, in fact, best read as plotting a middle way between the complaisant endorsement of modern technology, on the one hand, and the Luddite demand for a return to the cave, on the other. It is when, however, Heidegger turns to the question of what we are to do about the devastation of our world, how we are to bring about this turning to a new age, that his thinking becomes especially distinctive, challenging and, to some readers, even offensive. The reason for this is his introduction of what, provisionally (and, as we will see, ultimately inaccurately) we may call the 'fatalism' theme.

2. *Gestell*, says Heidegger, though it is 'accomplished' *through*, is not accomplished *by* human beings. It is not the product of human intention, not 'human handiwork' (QCT p. 18). No individual, and no 'committee' (QCT p. 23) either, determines the character of modernity's understanding of reality. Conspiracy theories about world-disclosure are always false. Rather, like all those other disclosures which define the epochs that add up to ('world') history, *Gestell* is a 'destining [*Geschick*]' (QCT p. 24) which is 'sent', 'destined' (*ibid.*) or 'granted' to man (QCT pp. 31–2) by Being. Like every other epochal world-disclosure, *Gestell* is a 'destining of B/being' (TT p. 38). Human beings are always receptive rather than creative with respect to world-disclosure.

Because of this, and because, too, the only way to abolish *Gestell* (short of abolishing ourselves) would be to create a new world-disclosure to take its place, we lack the power to abolish the destitution that *Gestell* brings. *Gestell,* says Heidegger, 'will never allow itself to be mastered either positively or negatively by a human doing' (TT p. 38) but is something, rather, that 'holds complete sway over man', reigns as a kind of 'fate' (QCT p. 25). It follows that 'human activity can never...counter the danger', that 'human achievement...can never banish it' (QCT p. 33). 'No single man, no group of men, no commission of prominent statesmen can break or direct the progress of history' in the present age (DT p. 52). All we can do is to 'wait' upon the arrival of a new unveiling of reality to redeem the fallen state of our culture: 'Man['s]...essence is to be the one who waits' (TT p. 42). Not 'human thought and endeavor', then, but rather, 'only a god can save us' (S p. 107).

This is the 'fatalist' conclusion that many of his critics have discovered in Heidegger and found to be offensive. According to Winifred Franzen, for example,

While in *Being and Time* there had been in principle no subject of history...now [in Heidegger's later philosophy] Being itself was elevated to the rank of absolute subject of history and man condemned to total subjection to history and its fateful sendings.[1]

Again, Richard Wolin claims that the central thrust of Heidegger's later philosophy is to place us in 'impotent bondage'[2] to Being, a retrospective attempt, Wolin suggests, to expunge his own and Germany's war guilt by attributing the course of history to the workings of impersonal and supra-human forces. And even someone as indebted in his own thinking to Heidegger as Karsten Harries, criticizes severely what he takes to be the fatalist character of Heidegger's thought. Its portrayal of us as the victims and spectators of history means, he claims, that Heidegger's later philosophy 'precludes every attempt to build from the ruins of our culture a house in which we can dwell',[3] renders every effort to transform or ameliorate our condition futile.

---

[1] *Von der Existenz-ontologie zur Seinsgeschichte* (Meisenheim: Hein, 1975) p. 125.
[2] *The Politics of Being: the political Thought of Martin Heidegger* (Cambridge: MIT Press, 1993) p. 151.
[3] '*Verwahrloste Welt*' in *Kunst-Politik-Technik*, eds. C. Jamme and K. Harries (Munich: Fink, 1993) p. 215.

In order to assess whether Heidegger's position really is as objectionable as these critics assert we need to understand, first, why he denies 'human activity' the power to 'master', that is, abolish, *Gestell,* and, second, whether this denial really does entail the futility of *all* redemptive action. I shall discuss these issues in the order presented.

3. Why does Heidegger deny to 'human achievement' (QCT p. 33), to 'a human doing founded merely on itself' (TT p. 38), the power to redeem us from our 'destitution'? Why does he think the turning to a post-modern age to be something which, even with the best will in the world, we cannot *make* happen?

In the previous chapter I emphasized that *Gestell* is not a simple but rather a complex two-part phenomenon. It comprises (a) modernity's version of the technological disclosure of B/being, its way of disclosing things as resource, and (b) the metaphysical misinterpretation of (a) which 'drives out every other possibility of revealing' and so results in the 'illusion' that things are *nothing but* resource. The *radix malorum* in *Gestell,* I emphasized, is not (a) but rather (b). It follows, we saw, that 'the turning' will consist not in the breaking of machines but in the overcoming of metaphysical illusion, the 'clearing of the clearing', that will allow things to show up once more in their sacred 'ownness' and so require of us that we become once more their 'guardians'.

4. Given this understanding of the nature of the turning it becomes relatively obvious why we cannot *make* the new post-modern, post-metaphysical age happen.

'Everything', says Heidegger, 'depends on this: that we ponder', that we engage in the kind of thinking which allows, 'the . . . arising of the saving power' (QCT p. 32). Only through thinking can 'salvation' happen. What kind of thinking does Heidegger have in mind?

One kind of thinking is what (in chapter 1 section 9) I call philosophical, and Heidegger 'meditative' thinking (DT p. 53), the thinking we have been engaged in throughout this book. Heidegger says that 'instead of merely staring at the technological' (and perhaps 'cursing it as the work of the devil') we must 'above all . . . catch sight of . . . the essence of [modern] technology' (QCT p. 32). This catching sight, he says, 'brings into appearance the saving power in its arising' (QCT p. 28). This is why we can say, with Hölderlin, that '...where the danger is, grows / The saving power also' (QCT p. 28).

The point, I think, is this. Once we have brought the essence of modern technology, *Gestell*, properly into view, and once we have seen, therefore, that it is merely one among innumerably many possibilities of disclosure – a disclosure which, however, modernity mistakenly absolutizes into what it takes to be the one and only true account of the nature of reality itself – then we see metaphysics for the 'illusion' (QCT p. 27) that it is and are thereby liberated from it. If, to produce a partial analogy, one comes to understand that the fact that one sees everything in shades of grey is due to a peculiarity of one's eyes which renders them insensible to every other colour in things, then one is liberated from the belief that the only colours things have are shades of grey. It is because meditation on the essence of modern technology liberates one from it that Heidegger calls that essence 'ambiguous [*zweideutig*]', Janus-faced (QCT p. 33). On the one hand, it is that which encages us in a world of godlessness, homelessness, and mindless violence. On the other, it is that which, pondered aright, 'points to the mystery of all revealing i.e. truth' (QCT p. 32), the 'mystery' (Being) being 'that which frees' (QCT p. 25).

Another kind of pondering which allows the 'arising of the saving power' (as we also saw in chapter 1 section 9) is 'poetic thinking', in other words, art. Heidegger holds that the art of great 'poets' such as Hölderlin, Rilke, Cézanne, Klee and the poets of Zen is art which 'founds the holy' (GA 52 p. 193, I p. 138, GA 4 p. 148). It is art which allows the 'unknown God' to shine forth in the sight of 'familiar' things (PMD p. 225), allows our world to stand forth as the self-disclosing *poiesis* of the self-concealing divinity. Art, too, the kind of art of which we are in particular need in the metaphysical age of modernity, 'points to the mystery of all revealing' and so frees us for a 'breakthrough to the Origin' (DK p. 213).[4]

5. 'Stone walls do not a prison make', runs the Stoic motto. Man's inalienable freedom lay, for the Stoics, in the fact that whatever the temporal powers might

---

[4] See HPA chapters 3 and 4. This is Heidegger's later conception of art, a conception he developed after he had got over the oppressive idea that the only valid kind of art is art which 'opens up a world' for 'an historical people' in the manner of the Greek temple or Medieval cathedral.

do to one's body, one's thoughts lie beyond its reach. Equally, on the other hand, stone walls, however well constructed, cannot make one's thoughts to be, in Heidegger's sense, free thoughts, thoughts that have been 'released' from metaphysics. And neither can the breaking of walls. The inaccessibility of (in the Rilkean language Heidegger sometimes uses) the 'inner space of the heart' (WPF pp. 129–30; compare WCT p. 144) in which one 'ponders' – or does not – the essence of truth, means that whatever external actions are performed, whatever social policies might be adopted by, for example, the state, they can never, in *Heidegger's* sense, make one free. The state may order the world in whatever way it likes – it might, as the Heidegger of 1934, crazed by the intoxication of Nazi power proposed, try to create a new clearing of being by destroying industrial civilization and replacing it with a pre-industrial form of life – but without the inner turn of the heart that 'clears' the clearing, all such action will be futile. As already remarked, one can be every bit as encaged by the misinterpretation of a primitive version of the technological disclosure of B/being as by the misinterpretation of the sophisticated version that belongs to modernity.[5] This need for the 'inner' turn is the reason *Gestell* can never be 'mastered'. Though there are many kinds of things social policy can, with sufficient resoluteness, 'master' – global warming, the AIDS epidemic, the population explosion – *Gestell* is not one of them. The reason is the inaccessibility of the inner domain to outer control.

For the 'change of heart' to affect our culture as a whole we are compelled, therefore, to 'wait'. Only a god can save us. The solution, that is to say (in one of the several meanings of this multi-layered utterance[6]), to the problem of technology lies beyond unaided human effort, can never, ultimately, be the product of 'human achievement'. It lies, as we say, 'in God's hands'. This is why 'The Turning' ends not with a call to action but with a kind of prayer:

---

[5] This is the reason, I think, why most of those who 'dropped out' in the 1960s dropped back in again. Sensing the spiritual poverty of the age, many of those associated with the hippie movement sought to escape such poverty by returning to the rural, handicraft world of pre-modern life. What they mostly missed, however, was that the root of that poverty was 'nothing technological', nothing that could be cured by external change alone.

[6] The other meanings are, I suggest: (1) Only when the 'unknown God' of the poets shows himself in the sight of 'familiar' things will we overcome metaphysics and (2) Only when we are united by communal worship of a 'god' (or pantheon of 'gods') will we be, in the full sense, once more a community.

May world in its worlding be the nearest of all nearing that nears, as it brings the truth of Being near to man's essence, and so gives man to belong to the disclosing bringing-to-pass that is a bringing into its own. (TT p. 49)

6. But, to repeat the accusation of fatalism, however well-founded they might be, do not these reflections still reduce us to impotent spectators, the victims rather than makers of history? Is it not indeed the case that they render 'every attempt to build from the ruins of our culture a house in which we can dwell' utterly futile?

Heidegger anticipates and rejects this criticism. Though *Gestell* is, indeed, a kind of 'fate', one that holds 'complete sway' over us, it is 'never a fate that compels' (QCT p. 25). Again, that *Gestell* is something 'destined' to us means, he says, 'something different from the talk we hear more and more frequently to the effect that technology is the fate of our age, where "fate" means "the inevitability of an unalterable course" (QCT p. 25). And that *Gestell* is a destining 'in no way confines us to a stultifying compulsion to push on blindly with technology or, which comes to the same thing, to rebel helplessly against it and curse it as the work of the devil' (QCT p. 27).

How are we to understand these remarks? On the one hand we cannot abolish *Gestell* – abolish that which is described in the *second* clause of its definition – so that we are obliged to inhabit it as long as 'history' decrees this to be so. On the other hand we are not 'compelled' to 'push on blindly' with the way things are, a state of things the persistence of which is by no means 'inevitable'. Why is this not a contradiction? Because, evidently, though we cannot *make Gestell* disappear there are things we can do which *encourage* it to do so, a fact which enables us to live in hope, 'summon[s] us to hope in the growing light of the saving power' (QCT p. 33).

What are these things? We know already. 'Everything depends on this': that we engage in the poetic and meditative thinking that allows the 'flourish[ing]' of 'releasement to the things and openness to the mystery' (DT p. 56). If we engage in such thinking then we withdraw ourselves from the 'enframed' life of mainstream modernity, engage in a kind of 'emigration' that takes us away from the violent and dis-enchanted centre of our culture and relocates us at its margins. We become, in other words, in Nietzsche's sense, 'untimely' – the condition in which, according to Heidegger, 'essential' thinking has always found itself (IM p. 8). If we engage in such thinking 'persistent[ly] and coura-geous[ly]' (DT p. 56), if it takes hold of and shapes our lives, then we take the 'step back' out of metaphysics and 'find our way back into the full breadth of the space proper to our essences'. We become, in other words, beings who dwell. But otherwise we do not.

Quietism?

7. Let us distinguish what I shall call 'the world turning', the turning of our culture as a whole to a new, post-modern, post-metaphysical age, from 'the personal turning', the turning of the thought and life of an individual such as that Heidegger identifies as beginning in his own life in 1930. Using this distinction we may, it seems, summarize Heidegger's position as follows. Though we cannot make the world turning happen, each of us has the power, like Socrates, to place our own lives in the pure 'draft' of ever-'withdrawing' Being (WCT pp. 350–1) and thereby transform our being-in-the-world from homelessness into dwelling. What follows is that the charge of fatalism is defeated. Since we can all 'think', we are, at least where our personal histories are concerned, far from being reduced to 'impotent spectators of history'.

This, however, it may be said, is a very small victory. For all that has been achieved is to draw our attention to the fact that a doctrine of 'fatalism' may apply to either of two domains: one may be a fatalist either about the life of a culture as a whole or about the lives of the individuals who inhabit it. True, the critic now concedes, Heidegger is not fatalistic about the latter. Yet he still remains completely so about the former. It follows that what he recommends is a form of quietism: a kind of Stoic retreat, a withdrawal of all active concern for one's fellows and one's culture as a whole. What Heidegger recommends – all that he allows to be possible – is that we withdraw into our private worlds, pull up the drawbridge, and leave it to 'God' to take care of the rest. In sum, therefore, we must conclude that after losing his faith in Nazism, like many of his countrymen who rejected Nazism but felt helpless (or too afraid) to do anything about it, Heidegger withdrew into a kind of 'inner emigration' from which he never emerged.

Clearly, if this charge is to be defeated, if the possibility of the personal turn is to 'summon us to hope' for the condition of our culture as a whole, there must be some link between the personal turning and the world turning. But Heidegger maintains that there is such a link. To make the personal turn to dwelling *is*, 'here and now and in little things, . . . [to] foster the saving power in its increase' (QCT p. 33). After some necessary preparation in chapters 7 and 8, I shall turn to the task of understanding why this should be so in chapter 9.

7   The ethics of dwelling

1. The 'world turning' to a new, post-metaphysical, age is something, we saw in the previous chapter, we cannot *make* happen. We cannot 'master' history. On the other hand, however, we can, each of us, make the 'personal turning'. And rather than being a 'quietistic' withdrawal from active concern for the spiritual health of our culture as a whole, Heidegger claims, the personal turning to dwelling is (in a perhaps necessarily modest way) a 'fostering' of the world turning. Why should this be so? To answer this question we need to begin by asking: what actually is it to make the turn to dwelling? What is it to dwell?

2. In a way, of course, we have answered this question already (in chapter 4). For we know already that to dwell is, first, to be cared-for, ultimately 'safe', in the dwelling place, and, second, to care-for the things of the dwelling place, to be their 'guardian'. But just what is it to be a 'guardian'? It is on this question that I wish to focus in this and the following chapter.

Notice, first of all, something exciting about the connexion Heidegger makes between dwelling and guardianship. Since the time of the Greeks, the most fundamental of all requests that have been made of philosophy is the request for an account of 'the good life'; an account that is grounded not in human subjectivity, not in taste, intuition or custom, but in, rather, reflective insight into the nature of reality itself. Put into Hume's language, the request is for a fundamental 'ought' that is as securely anchored in humanity-independent reality as is any 'is', an 'ought' that we simply *discover*, and in no sense *make*, to be the case. Though strongly averse to being cast in the role of a guru and so doing his best to disguise it, Heidegger's meditation on dwelling, in fact, it seems to me, provides such an account.

Dwelling, that is to say 'essential' dwelling (see chapter 4 section 9), is the human 'essence'. Even if we are oblivious to the fact, we all live in a holy world, a world, that is to say, which is to be cared-for. Whether we know it or not, this is the *truth* of the matter. It follows that we *are* the guardians of B/being – in fact its sole guardians – whether we practise that guardianship or not. As respect, reverence and celebration is the proper way of being in a church – whether we practise this or not – so guardianship is our proper, our 'fitting' (I p. 82) way of being-in-the-world, our task as human beings, whether or not we are conscious of that task and whether or not we live up to it.

Hence the title of this chapter: from Heidegger's meditations on B/being, truth and the human essence that we have examined in previous chapters arises an account of 'the good life', an 'ethics', an ethics that is centred on the notion of guardianship.

Of course, no 'ethics' really arises from the meditation we have conducted so far, alone. Ethics is concerned with action, with, more generally, *praxis* (refraining from acting as well as acting). It is concerned with providing us with a procedure, or at least guidelines, for determining how we are to act. But 'Understand the holiness of things!', 'Become a guardian!', tell us nothing more than 'Be nice!'; in other words, at the level of action, nothing at all. What we need, for our meditation to become a genuine ethics, is to supplement it in some way that will bridge the gap between the abstract generality of 'Be a guardian!' and the level of concrete particularity at which human decisions about action actually occur.

By way of bridging this gap, it seems to me, Heidegger provides two things. First, a taxonomical account of the essential features of the object of caring-for and, second, a taxonomical account of caring-for itself. These together, I shall suggest, while providing nothing like an algorithm of action along the lines intended by, for example, Kant's categorical Imperative, are sufficiently directive at the level of action to justify my claim that there is, in later Heidegger, a genuine 'ethics'.

Heidegger's answer to the question 'What is the to-be-cared-for?' is 'the fourfold (*das Geviert*)' (BDT p. 150). His answer to 'What is caring-for?' is that 'it is something *positive* and takes place when we leave something beforehand in its own nature' or when we 'set something free into its own presencing' (BDT pp. 149–50). I shall discuss these answers in the order presented.

The fourfold

3. To understand dwelling as guardianship of 'the fourfold' we need to understand 'the fourfold'.

'The fourfold' is later Heidegger's account of 'world' (T p. 179). It is the world one inhabits in so far as one dwells. To dwell, says Heidegger, is to 'belong... within the fourfold of sky and earth, mortals and divinities' (TT p. 49, BDT p. 150). Since all humans dwell in the 'essential' sense (see chapter 4 section 9), all inhabit the fourfold. Only, however, to those who dwell in the 'existential' sense does it show up *as* the fourfold. Existential dwelling is, we may say, 'experienc[ing] and tak[ing] over' (LH p. 257) the fourfold in its fourfoldness.

In *Being and Time* Heidegger conceives human ('Dasein's') 'being-in-the-world' as a structural concept to be elucidated by means of an elucidation of the elements of this structure. He calls these structural, necessary or *a priori* features of human existence 'existentials'. The structure as a whole he refers to as 'care [*Sorge*]' which he defines in terms of the threefold structure of Dasein's 'temporality'. Care, that is to say, is Dasein's involvement in a *present* world of 'equipment' (or the 'ready-to-hand') and other Dasein, an involvement which is conditioned by the legacy of a cultural *past* ('heritage'), a legacy which provides Dasein with the outline of the proper projection of its life into the *future*.

Though I have been concerned, in the main, to emphasize the strong discontinuity between *Being and Time* and later Heidegger, to emphasize that the 'turn' that separates them is a *Kehre* (U-turn) rather than a *Wende* (curve), I want now to bring to the fore an important point of continuity. Later, like earlier, Heidegger conceives of being-in-the-world (whether a dwelling or a 'homeless' mode of being) as a structural concept to be elucidated *via* the elements of the structure. Being 'on the earth', 'under the sky', among men ('mortals'), and 'before the divinities' (BDT p. 149) are the 'existentials' (though Heidegger no longer uses this language) that make up this structure. How and to what extent, I want now to ask, does later Heidegger's four-fold structure of existentials map onto the threefold structure of *Being and Time*?

'Earth'[1] and 'sky', in some sense of the term, clearly, 'nature', correspond to nothing in *Being and Time*'s threefold structure. In that early work the environment in which human beings find themselves is the interconnected

---

[1] It is very important not to confuse the 'earth' of 'The Origin of the Work of Art' with the 'earth' of the fourfold. The former, as we have seen, is the mystery of the unconcealed, the 'Dionysian'. With respect to the fourfold, however, as we shall see, the mystery is, as it were, distributed equally between its four elements.

network of the 'ready-to-hand'. Nature, in so far as it appears at all, differs from artifacts merely in the fact that it is ready-made equipment: the wind shows up in Dasein's world as and only as – as *nothing but* – 'wind-in-the-sails' or a sign of approaching rain, animals as, and only as, ready-made food and clothing. Later Heidegger, however, rejects this, as one might well think, writing of *Gestell* into the *universal* structure of human existence. Whether we know and are moved by the fact or not, that which environs us, our equipment, and our social and productive networks, is 'earth' and 'sky', 'nature' in a sense of the term which, we are about to see, cannot possibly be subsumed under 'equipment'.[2]

'Mortals', by contrast, clearly does find an echo in the earlier structure. It corresponds to the (essentially mortal) 'Dasein' of *Being and Time*. As early Heidegger identifies being among other Dasein, '"being-with-others" [*Mitsein*]', as an existential, so late Heidegger identifies 'belonging to men's being-with-one-another [*gehörend in das miteinander der Menschen*]' (PLT p. 149) as an essential feature of the structure of being-in-the-world.

The gods

4. The element in late Heidegger's understanding of being-in-the-world that is most difficult to comprehend is 'the gods'.[3] Who are Heidegger's gods? In 'Building Dwelling Thinking' and its companion piece, 'The Thing'

---

[2] At one point (BT 70) *Being and Time* does acknowledge that 'the nature which 'stirs and strives', which assails us and enthralls us as landscape' remains 'hidden' from the analysis of nature as ready-made equipment. Had Heidegger paid more attention to this anomaly, rather than simply recording its existence and passing on, the turn to the later thinking might have occurred much sooner.

[3] Much of the time Heidegger prefers to talk of 'the divinities [*die Göttlichen*]' rather than 'the gods [*die Götter*]'. The distinction should not, however, be overly stressed since it is neither universal nor systematic. Insofar as there is a point to the preference – apparent, for example, in 'Building Dwelling Thinking's statement of the fourfold (BDT p. 150) – it is, I think, to move us away from thinking of 'the gods' as resembling those of any familiar religion or theology. It is a mistake to suppose that Heidegger's 'return of the gods' necessarily entails the return of anything resembling organized religion as it has hitherto manifested itself.

   A further point about 'the gods': they are not, to repeat, on any account, to be confused with the 'God' which, in chapter 1, I argued Heideggerian Being to be, since while the former are beings the latter – emphatically – is 'something completely and utterly other' than any being. This 'God', as we are about to see, does not belong among, but is, rather, a precondition of 'the gods'. More exactly, opennes to 'God', to 'the holy', ' the divine', the 'unknown' God of the poets (PMD p. 225), is the precondition of 'the gods' of the fourfold being *living* gods, gods that make a difference to our lives.

(T pp. 165–82),[4] the divinities are described as 'messengers' (BDT p. 150, T p. 178), a point made in the later Hölderlin discussions by calling them, with Hölderlin, 'angels': 'the angel is the essence of what we otherwise call "the gods" more purely expressed' (GA 4 p. 20).[5] What, however, is the 'message' that they bring?

For Heidegger the gods are always closely associated with what he variously call the divine 'destinings' (QCT p. 34), 'laws' (HE p. 312) or 'edicts' (I p. 116). He says, for example, that Greek tragedy 'brought the presence of the gods, [i.e.] brought the dialogue of divine and human destinings to radiance' (QCT p. 34). In some sense, the gods *are* the 'divine destinings'.

The divine laws of a community are what 'The Origin of the Work of Art' refers to as the 'simple and essential decisions' (OWA p. 48) granted to it by history, its fundamental understanding of the proper way for it to be, both collectively and individually, its fundamental *ethos*. (See further HPA Chapter 1 sections 14–15.) The divine laws provide the standard against which state law is ultimately to be judged. Antigone's resistance to the merely 'human statutes' of Creon's state, for example, is justified by – here Heidegger quotes Sophocles – 'the immutable, unwritten edict divine' (I p. 116). Moreover, the divine laws are the basis for a critique of current public opinion: they 'tend both towards and away from' 'the voice of the people' (HE p. 312).

Though occasionally inclining to the view that the divine laws are 'of the gods' in the sense of being understood as being *sanctioned* by them (at, for example, GA 4 p. 126), Heidegger's final (and certainly best[6]) view is that they are 'of the gods' in the sense of being announced to us, given 'voice', by the

---

[4] The two essays were published simultaneously in volume II of *Vorträge und Aufsätze* and display a considerable overlap in both content and language.

[5] Notice that angels, Rilke's (WPF pp. 134–5) or Wim Wenders', for example, are bearers of tidings rather than possessors of power. Angels rarely perform miracles. (In Wender's *Far away, so Close*, for example, Cassio can only save a child's life, alter history, *via* incarnation, by 'becoming man'.) Angels do, of course, possess a kind of power, the power of charisma, but this is a natural power, not the power to suspend the laws of nature. We should thus expect the same to be true of Heidegger's gods.

[6] In the *Euthophro*, Plato makes the decisive point that since it always makes sense to ask (particularly of the *Greek* gods) 'Is what the gods love good?', the 'good' cannot be *defined* as that which is loved by the gods since then the question would reduce to the idiocy 'Do the gods love what they love?' (G. E. Moore later re-presented this as the so-called 'open question argument'.) In the Old Testament, of course, what is to be done *is* sometimes defined as God's command. Abraham is to sacrifice his son Isaac for no reason other than that – inexplicably – God commands it. As Kierkegaard points out, however, this marks Abraham as living, not the 'ethical' life, but something else which he dubs the 'religious' life.

'messenger' gods (GA 4 p. 169). Since, however, the laws are 'unwritten' (I p. 116), the gods – unlike Moses – cannot properly articulate them in words. They communicate them, rather, by being embodiments, incarnations or *exemplars* of the laws. They communicate them not, or not primarily, by *saying*, but rather by *showing* – by being the beings who they are.[7]

In *Being and Time* Heidegger speaks of the 'existence possibilities' embodied in 'heritage' as the 'sole authority' acknowledged by a 'free being', the authority that provides the basis for a critical assessment of the practices of the current 'One', the practices validated by contemporary public opinion (BT 391). He also holds that these 'existence possibilities' are personified in the figures of 'heroes' which are memorialized in the collective memory of a culture. Hence living autonomously, 'authentically', is a matter of Dasein's committing itself to its 'hero', that is to say, committing itself to 'loyally following in the footsteps' of those of the exemplary heroes of its culture that are appropriate to its own particular situation (BT 385, 391).

These parallels make it clear, I think, that the 'divine laws' of later Heidegger correspond to the 'existence possibilities' preserved as 'heritage' of early Heidegger, and that 'the gods' of late Heidegger are the reincarnations of early Heidegger's 'heroes'.[8] If this is correct then the important point to notice is that since heritage (as part of what *Being and Time* calls the cultural 'thrownness' within which Dasein always finds itself situated) is an

---

[7] 'Building Dwelling Thinking' says that the divinities are messengers 'of the godhead' (BDT p. 150) (again, I think, not to be confused with the 'God' I discussed in chapter 1). The principle feature of a 'godhead' is *unity*. The Christian godhead, for example, is 'three in one and one in three'. Heidegger uses the term, I believe, to stress the necessary unity of anything that can count as a communal *ethos*. A group cannot count as a community, as sharing, in Heidegger's sense, a common culture if, for example, half of it acknowledges only gods of war and pillage, the other half only gods of peace and learning. (This is not to deny that within the same community there may be gods, say, for men and gods for women, only to say that, taken together, the gods must represent a coherently unified form of life.)

[8] In '*Hölderlin's Erde und Himmel*' Heidegger disclaims originality with respect to the fourfold. Though not named as such, it is, nonetheless, he says, fully present in Hölderlin (GA 4 pp. 170–1). This implies that the elements of the fourfold are taken from Hölderlin, that its gods, in particular, are identical with Hölderlin's gods. And certainly, as we have seen (section 6 above), the idea of the god as an 'angel', a charismatic ethical messenger rather than possessor of supernatural power, Heidegger indeed takes from Hölderlin. At the same time, however, if I am right, a Nietzschean influence must also be recognized. For, as *Being and Time* explicitly acknowledges (BT p. 396), the idea of the exemplary 'hero', the 'role-' or, better, 'life- model', is taken from Nietzsche's 'On the Uses and Abuses of History', from, specifically, his conception of the 'memorializing' function of history. Later Heidegger's conception of the gods is actually, I would suggest, something of a synthesis of Hölderlinian and Nietzschean ideas.

existential feature of human being so, too, are the gods. Living 'before the divinities' (BDT p. 149) is something we *always* do whether we acknowledge it or not – as long, at least, as we remain, in the full sense, *human* beings.

This point becomes impossible to grasp if one equates late Heidegger's talk of modernity as the age of the 'default' or 'absence' of the gods with Nietzsche's talk of the 'death of God', with his view of modernity as the age that has suffered the *extermination* of the divinities. In fact, however, 'default' is clearly not to be equated with 'death' since Heidegger speaks, for example, of that paradigm of modernity, the motorway (freeway) bridge, as 'a passage which crosses before the divinities' (BDT p. 153). The gods, therefore, must be *present* in modernity even though, as with the bridge, 'their presence is obstructed . . . even pushed wholly aside' (*ibid.*). Gods, in modernity, are not dead. They are merely 'withdrawn into concealment' (BDT p. 150). Heidegger makes this explicit in the following passage:

The default of God and the divinities is absence. But absence is not nothing. [The non-existent cannot be 'absent'.] Rather it is precisely the presence, which must first be appropriated, of the hidden fullness and wealth of what has been and what, thus gathered, is presencing, of the divine in the world of the Greeks, in prophetic Judaism, in the preaching of Jesus. This no-longer is in itself a not-yet of the veiled arrival of its inexhaustible nature. (T p. 184)

In modernity, then, the gods remain with us. But they are not 'appropriated' into our lives, do not 'dispose the world's history' (WPF p. 91), fail, speaking of the culture as a whole, to make a difference to what actually happens in the world.

Why are the gods absent, concealed, in modernity? Concealment, for Heidegger, is always lack of illumination. The concealed 'side' of the 'globe of being', for example, is the 'dark' side, that which is unilluminated. Similarly, as we saw in chapter 2 (sections 5–6), the concealment of the gods is due to the absence of the 'divine radiance' (WPF p. 91). The gods, when they appear, appear 'out of the holy sway' (WPF p. 150) so as to be 'remove[d] from any comparison' with ordinary beings (T p. 178). Later Heidegger's gods, that is, are not just the 'messengers' of the divine laws but are charismatic, inspiring, and so *authoritative*, messengers.[9] Yet since modernity has lost its

---

[9] For Heidegger the nature of ultimate ethical authority is charismatic. That which motivates us to do the good is always, as we have seen, its holiness. This post-enlightenment understanding of the character of ethical authority is, of course, *dangerous*. It is what made it possible for

sense of the sacred, has become closed off from 'the holy', that 'aether' in which alone gods can appear as gods, it provides no 'abode' in which its gods could take up residence (WPF p. 94). The gods are absent because we live in the age of 'metaphysics', of dis-enchantment, the age of the victory of the prosaic over the poetic.

5. The gods of the fourfold correspond, then, to the 'heroes' of *Being and Time*. They embody – are – heritage, and as such are existential features of our lives, our being-in-the-world. As human beings, whatever we do, whatever bridges we construct, we do and construct 'before the divinities'. It seems, then, that late Heidegger's account of being-in-the-world is given in terms of four 'existential' elements: as humans, we live our lives on (a part of) the planet ('earth'), in a particular climate ('sky'), among human beings ('mortals') and under the (appropriated or unappropriated) guidance of a particular ethical heritage ('gods'). (Alternatively put, since sky and earth add up, evidently, to nature, and mortals together with their gods to culture, we might say that human being-in-the-world is being-in the – of course 'interconnected' (AWP p. 129) – 'twofold' of nature and culture.)

There is, however, a problem with the account of the fourfold as so far presented. Though, as we have seen, every human being dwells, inhabits the fourfold in the 'essential' sense, only those who dwell in the 'existential' sense 'take over and experience' that habitation, only to them does the fourfold show up *as* the fourfold. Since, as we have also seen, lack of existential dwelling is the defining condition of modernity, it follows that the fourfold does *not* show up as the fourfold to 'homeless' (LH p. 258, BDT p. 161) modernity. Yet that we live on a part of the planet, in a particular climate, among other human beings in a society with a particular ethical tradition is hardly occult knowledge. It is how our existence reveals itself, how the world shows up, to *everyone*. It follows that something must be missing from my description

Heidegger, for a time, to think of Hitler as a new god and is why, having recovered himself, he warns against the worship of 'idols' and manufactured gods (BDT p. 150). A crucial task, therefore, is that of distinguishing between true gods and false idols. It would be nice, perhaps, if, as Kant dreamt, 'reason' supplied us with rules, algorithms, for doing this. But, such is life, there are none. As the Greeks understood, and Heidegger emphasizes in the Rilke essay, life is essentially a *Wagnis*, a 'venture' or 'risk', in which illusion – 'dissembling' (OWA p. 54) – constantly threatens to conceal truth. All we can do is to try to determine, to the best of our ability, whether a putative god belongs in the company of the acknowledged gods, whether it really is an embodiment of the 'divine destinings'.

of the fourfold, something that makes the difference between (existential) dwelling[10] and its lack. There must be more to the fourfold than has so far met the eye.

Here is Heidegger's own description of the elements of the fourfold:

> earth is the serving bearer blossoming and fruiting, spreading out in rock and water, rising up in plant and animal . . . The sky is the vaulting path of the sun, the course of the changing moon, the wandering glitter of the stars, the year's seasons and their changes, the light and dusk of day, the gloom and glow of night, the clemency and inclemency of the weather, the drifting clouds and blue depth of the aether . . . The divinities are the beckoning messengers of the godhead . . . The mortals are human beings. They are called mortals because they . . . are capable of death as death. (BDT p. 150)

Of, that is, understanding it as the 'shrine' of the presencing of the 'mystery of Being itself' (T p. 178).

The difference between this and my prosaic description of the fourfold being-in-the-world is surely obvious. Whereas I employed the prosaic words of astronomy, meteorology, biology and sociology, Heidegger employs the radiant, words of poetry.[11] And he does so not as casual literary hyperbole but rather to *show* something. What he shows, surely, in his saying of the fourfold, is what it is to dwell. To dwell, he shows, is to inhabit 'the poetic' (PMD p. 228): it is for the existential structure of being-in-the-world to light up poetically, for it to become transparent to Being, for the 'unknown' God to come to presence in 'the sight of . . . what is familiar to man' (PMD p. 225). What Heidegger shows is that, in Hölderlin's words, 'poetically man dwells' (PMD p. 213–29).

One dwells when one's world shows up poetically, 'radiantly', when it shows up as the 'holy' place that it is. (One dwells when one's experience of it becomes an '*Ereignis*-experience'.) But one's world is a fourfold structure. So one dwells when that fourfold structure lights up, when the planet becomes 'earth', when sky becomes 'the heavens' (the German '*Himmel*' covers both

---

10 From now on I shall generally drop the 'existential' on the understanding 'dwelling', without qualification, always to mean 'existential dwelling'.

11 Heidegger has an interesting and important account of the 'radiance' of poetry. Very roughly, whereas the prosaic word is '*eindeutig*', possessed of only one meaning, the genuinely poetic word is '*vieldeutig*', possessed of many meanings. The poetic word 'vibrates' with an 'inexhaustible richness' of semantic 'spaces', spaces which spread out through, but also in a certain sense *beyond*, the categories of everyday intelligibility. Authentic poetry thus, in a certain sense that is not to be confused with representation, brings 'the mystery' to presence *in* its mystery, brings to presence that which is concealed by the disclosure in which we live out the 'everydayness' of our lives (see HPA chapter 3 section 17).

meanings), when men become 'mortals', and when the existence possibilities of heritage become radiant 'divinities'. This is the connexion between
Heidegger's two central statements about dwelling, 'poetically man dwells'
and 'dwelling is inhabiting the fourfold'. The latter is the explication, the
fully established meaning, of the former.

6. As *praxis*, we have seen, dwelling is guardianship of, caring-for, 'the
abode', our world. That world is, however, the fourfold. Hence, dwelling
is caring-for the fourfold. But that means that caring-for is four-aspected:
'the caring-for that dwells is fourfold' (BDT p. 150). Dwelling is caring-for
earth, sky, gods and mortals.

Which earth, sky, gods and mortals? *Which* four-aspected world is the object
of caring-for? First and foremost, Heidegger argues, a *local* world. For the
places in which people dwell are *local* worlds, local fourfolds.

One's dwelling-place, observes Heidegger, is somewhere that is 'near' to
one, somewhere where one is 'in the nearness'. (His word here is '*die Nähe*' –
which also means 'the neigbourhood' i.e. dwelling-place.) In the essay on
Hölderlin's 'Homecoming' Heidegger defines the *Heimat* (home, homeland)
as the '*Land der Nähe*', the 'land of nearness' (GA 4 p. 28). But nearness
implies farness, fails to 'appear' if 'remoteness . . . remains absent' (T p. 166).
The 'homely' (in the sense of the German *heimish*) implies the foreign.
Heidegger makes the same point by pointing out that, unlike mathematical
space, dwelling spaces are always finite, bounded: space (*Raum* – which also
means 'room') in its original meaning of 'place cleared or freed for settlement'
is 'cleared and free . . . within a boundary', a boundary being 'not where something stops but . . . that from which something *begins its presencing*' (BDT
p. 154).[12] One of the central dangers of modern communications technology
is that it threatens to create a 'uniform distancelessness' (T p. 166) where
everything is equally near and equally remote. Even those who remain in
their traditional homelands become uprooted from the place which can speak
to them poetically because what comes 'closer' to them is the 'world that is
no world' (the 'virtual' world) presented to them by 'radio and television',
'picture magazines' (DT p. 48) and, of course, one must add, the Internet.

---

[12] The boundary of a dwelling-place may, of course, be fuzzy. There is no exact spot where the
East End stops and the rest of London starts, no sharp line separating the American Mid-West
from the East. Yet the East End is a different place from the rest of London, the Mid-West from
the East.

7. Heidegger's principle that homeliness implies foreignness seems intuitively plausible. To be truly at home in one place, it seems plausible to say, is for one to be not – or at least less[13] – at home in other places. Someone who is as much at home in any one place as any other, one wants to say, is at home *nowhere*. Such a person is not a universal dweller but rather a nomad[14] or, in Heidegger's language, an 'adventurer' (I p. 74, GA 52 p. 181). (One thinks here, perhaps, of the professorial hero of David Lodge's *Changing Places* who announces that the true home of the successful academic is the international airport.) It is worth asking, however, why we should accept Heidegger's principle. What argument can be given to show that the idea of a universal dweller is an impossible one?

What needs to be emphasized is that a dwelling space is not just a region of physical space. It is, rather, an interconnected complex of natural and cultural features which adds up to the notion of *place*. By 'interconnected' I have in mind what Heidegger calls the 'mirror-play' or 'ring dance' of the fourfold (T pp. 179–80), the idea that each of its elements is logically or conceptually related to each of the others. In cooler climates, to take just one example, one grows grain not grapes. But this entails that festive practices associated with the harvesting and processing of grapes cannot be part of a culture that belongs to such a climate. Different customs, different 'gods', in Heidegger's language, those associated with beer rather than wine, will belong to Northern places, to Northern 'earths' and 'skies'.

To be at home in, to belong to a place, as we know, is for it to show up as a holy, a 'poetic' place. In particular, it is for the 'gods' of that place, the *ethos* of its people, to show up as holy, as, that is, authoritative. To belong to a place is to be committed to its *ethos*. Different places, however, house at least marginally different 'gods'. Hence the idea of being equally and fully at home everywhere threatens the unity of a person. It entails the possession of a multitude of different, and incompatible, fundamental commitments.[15] This

---

[13] Dwelling-places can be, and typically are, arranged like concentric circles. I can be most at home in my village, somewhat at home in my province, less at home in my country, and not at all at home out of it.

[14] Many so-called nomads, it should be noted, are, in the above sense, not nomads at all. The Australian Aborigines, for example, do (or did) not lack a homeland. They simply have an unusually large one within which they are unusually mobile.

[15] This means that one has to be careful to note that there is no 'equally' in Ralph Waldo Emerson's remark: 'To the poet, to the philosopher, to the saint, all things are friendly and sacred, all events profitable, all days holy, all men divine' (quoted by Nietzsche on the title page of the first edition of *The Gay Science*).

is why the putative 'universal dweller' *has* to be an 'adventurer', a person free of all commitments (save, perhaps, that of being an adventurer), like the hero of the stage version of Christopher Isherwood's Berlin stories, a mere 'camera'. And it is also why, though not impossible (Heidegger is guilty of sometimes suggesting that only the birthplace, only the land of one's *Blut und Boden*, can be a dwelling place), successful emigration is a slow and difficult process. What makes it difficult is that, though the change may be no more than a nuance, it entails and demands a change in personality. Changing places is changing people.

Conservation and *techne*

8. The object of the dweller's caring-for is, then, that localized and bounded place or world in which she dwells. Its 'dimensions' are earth,[16] sky, gods, and mortals.[17] What, however, of caring-for itself? In what does guardianship of the fourfold consist?

Heidegger says, to repeat, that caring-for is always 'something *positive*'. It happens either when we 'leave something beforehand in its own nature' (BDT p. 149) or when we 'free' something 'into its own presencing', 'bring it hither and forth' (SR p. 160). The same distinction is made in terms of 'saving [*retten*]' in 'the old sense still known to Lessing':

Saving does not only snatch something from a danger. To save really means to set something free into its own presencing. To save [for example] the earth is more than [not[18]] to exploit it or even wear it out. Saving the earth does not master the earth and does not subjugate it [in the manner of *Gestell*], which is merely one step from spoliation. (BDT p. 150)

These passages, it seems to me, distinguish two modes of caring-for, as I shall call them, the 'passive' and 'active' modes. These correspond to the two

---

[16] Christine Swanton has put to me the interesting question of where sea comes into the picture. The answer is that since 'earth is the serving bearer, blossoming and fruiting, spreading out in rock and water' sea, insofar as it is part of the homeland, is part of its 'earth'. We need to remember, however, that since the homeland is always bounded, not all of the sea is part of it. Typically, that enclosed within bays and harbours or adjacent to beaches will be such a part while the rest (where the 'rest' starts will likely be a fuzzy matter) will not be.

[17] And, of course, the holy. A dwelling-place conceived *à la* Heidegger is thus five-dimensional. Heidegger indeed calls the holy a 'dimension' – that which is 'measured' out by the poet (PMD pp. 220–1; see, too, LH p. 267).

[18] This 'not' is missing in the German text (VA II p. 24) but is obviously required by the sense.

different senses Heidegger attaches to the oft-repeated phrase 'letting be:'[19] ensuring that something is let alone, 'sparing and preserving', *conserving* it (quite different from ignoring it, which is why, even as conservation, caring-for is always 'positive'), and enabling what is potentially in being to come into actual being, 'freeing', for example, the figure slumbering in the marble.[20]

The above passages constitute a recapitulation and elaboration of the 'Greek' stance to B/being discussed in chapter 3 above. Let us briefly recall that discussion.

The 'Greeks', we know (those partially idealized beings constructed out of hints provided by the Greek language), understood the world as *poiesis*, 'bringing-forth', a bringing forth that divides into *physis*, unaided bringing forth, as when a mountain range comes into being or a bud bursts into flower, and *techne*, aided bringing-forth as when the artist, craftsman or thinker lends a hand to nature's 'blossoming'. The Greeks understood the world as 'nature's' (Being's) self-disclosure, the self-disclosure of a god, a god of mystery, might and majesty, but a god, too, thought of as possessing something of the nature of an artist. (Since *poiesis* means, as Heidegger points out, not merely 'bringing forth' but also 'poetry', the visible world, for the Greeks, is experienced as nature's 'poetry'.) *Physis* is where the artist-god realizes its intended design unaided, *techne* is where it requires human assistance or, better put, achieves its design through human agency. As *technites* the 'Greeks' thus conceived of themselves somewhat on the model of assistant workers co-operating with the artist-god in the production of a beautiful artwork.

Given this way of experiencing the world, passive caring-for, guardian-ship as conservation, becomes an essential aspect of one's mode of living. If the world, as a god's self-disclosure, is a holy place, a place radiant with the 'might of Being', 'touched by the exciting nearness of the fire of the heavens' (GA 39 p. 292), then one refrains, clearly, from altering or destroy-ing what are experienced as its fundamental or structural features – great rivers, mountains, forests, 'peoples', and so on. And clearly, too, when one does initiate world-changing action, when one engages in active caring-for

---

[19] Notice that the literal meaning of '*Gelassenheit*' is 'letting be'.

[20] I am not particularly happy with this 'active'-'passive' terminology since 'passive' obscures precisely what Heidegger insists on, the 'positive' character of *all* caring-for. Every other pair of terms I have been able to think of, however – at one stage I favoured 'conserving' versus 'creative' – has had even worse disadvantages, or else is linguistically cumbersome.

one's world, one seeks to articulate what is already implicit in the overall design of things. 'The Question concerning Technology' 's discussion of 'the four causes' gives, as we saw (in chapter 3 section 4), an example of such active caring-for. Unlike the modern manufacturer of, say, aluminium beer cans, the ancient silversmith 'considers carefully and gathers together' the silver, a range of designs, the human social practice of sacrifice and worship, and 'brings forth' what is implicit in them: a silver chalice. The same, says Heidegger, is true with respect to the Greek ship or house (QCT p. 13), an observation which anticipates, as we will see in the next chapter, much of Heidegger's thinking about the character of authentic architecture.

9. To 'dwell poetically', then, to stand in the 'Greek' experience of Being, to stand in a world 'touched by the exciting nearness of the fire of the heavens', is to stand in the 'festive' mood of awed and grateful 'wonder that around us a world worlds at all, that there is something rather than nothing', that there are things and we ourselves are in their midst, that we ourselves are' (GA 52 p. 64). And to stand in that mood/mode of world disclosure is to stand to things in a relation of active and passive guardianship, conservation and *techne*, that is directed in a 'fourfold' manner towards each of the four elements of the fourfold. How much information does this give us at the concrete and particular level of decision and action? And, to return to the question raised in section 2 above, does it yield enough information, is it sufficiently action-guiding, to justify my claim that Heidegger's account of dwelling as *praxis* amounts to an 'ethics'?

The way to answer this question is to look in concrete detail at what the life of dwelling works out to be; to look at the kinds of decisions and practices that dwelling commits us to in particular, concrete circumstances, in particular, at what kinds of changes in our current practices it might require of us. This investigation of what, in concrete detail, the *praxis* of dwelling comes to is the task for the next chapter.

8   Being a guardian

1. In this chapter, I want to show, in some detail, the kind of life that Heideggerian 'dwelling' is. My aim is to demonstrate, *via* concrete examples, that Heidegger's thinking about dwelling, his thinking about dwelling as the *praxis* of guardianship, while certainly no algorithm for generating the uniquely correct decision for every situation of practical choice, is nonetheless, as I claimed at the beginning of the previous chapter, sufficiently fertile – and sufficiently challenging – at the level of practical decision-making to count as a genuine 'ethics'.

2. The object of the dweller's caring-for is, we know, 'fourfold'. And caring-for is itself twofold. This provides an eightfold framework within which we may 'ponder the dwelling place' (LH p. 271), think about what, *in detail*, it means to dwell. I, however, wish to add a further complication to this already complicated schema.

The only place where Heidegger discusses the *praxis* of dwelling in anything like concrete detail is in relation to architecture. In the obscure but seminal[1] 'Building Dwelling Thinking', that is, Heidegger is concerned to discover what caring-for comes to insofar as one 'builds' – to discover, as one might put it, an 'ethics' of building. The discussion is conducted in terms of concrete examples of the kinds of things dwellers do build (the old bridge in Heidelberg, the Black Forest farmhouse) and the kinds of things they do not (the motorway bridge of modernity). In order to present Heidegger's discussion of building as the self-contained philosophy of architecture that it is, in order, that is, to keep it separate from my own attempts to develop his thinking into other regions of *praxis*, I shall therefore expand the above

---

[1] Seminal for, in particular, contemporary architects, a 'decisive text' in architecture schools according to Clive Dilnot's 'The Decisive Text: on Beginning to Read Heidegger's "Building Dwelling Thinking"' (*Harvard Architectural Review*, vol. 8, 1992) pp. 160–87. This, of itself, supports the view that there is a genuine ethics – an ethics, at least, of architecture – to be discovered in Heidegger.

eightfold into a sixteen-fold schema. In the case of each of the four elements of the fourfold I shall, that is, discuss, first non-architectural examples of passive caring-for that element, second non-architectural examples of actively caring-for it, third architectural examples of passively caring-for, and, finally, architectural examples of the active caring-for. Multiplied by four, the schema for the discussion that follows looks, therefore, like this:

	earth	sky	gods	mortals	
passive caring-for					} non-architectural
active caring-for					examples
passive caring-for					} architectural
active caring-for					examples

This may seem baroque. But it is only, it seems to me, by looking at Heideggerian thinking about dwelling in the exhaustive way implied by this schema that one is able to grasp the richness of its implications for life, to convince oneself that there really is an 'ethics' implicit in Heidegger's account of dwelling.

Caring-for 'earth'

3. Heidegger says, to repeat, that

Mortals dwell in that they save the earth – taking the word in the old sense still known to Lessing. Saving does not only snatch something from danger. To save really (*eigentlich*) means to set something free into its own presencing. To save the earth is more than [not] to exploit it or even wear it out. Saving the earth does not master the earth and does not subjugate it, which is merely one step from spoilation (BDT p. 150).

An example of *passive caring-for the earth*, of 'letting it be' in the sense of refraining from 'exploitation' and 'spoliation', might be striving for, and eventually being successful in having a forest or mountain range declared a national park or 'heritage' site. Other examples could be: recycling waste, using non-polluting fuels, protecting the creatures of the earth, threatened species, from extermination. Notice, to repeat, that passive caring-for, conserving, the earth is, as Heidegger says, something 'positive'. Letting it be is not *ignoring* it but rather the positive act of 'sparing and preserving'.

Active caring-for earth, remember, is 'letting it be' in the sense in which the sculptor 'lets be' the figure slumbering in the marble. It is (to borrow

Schopenhauer's description of the beauty of art) 'completing nature's only half-uttered words'. It seems to me that there are two ways in which something may fail fully to 'be', two ways in which nature may fail fully to express herself: either the thing in question has never been fully in being, or else what was once in being has its being diminished or destroyed by human (or occasionally natural) violence. In virtue of this second kind of lack of being one kind of active caring-for the things of the earth is letting them *once more* come fully into being. For example, replanting with natives a forest that has been decimated either by logging or by logging followed by the planting of exotics. Another example might be repopulating forests that have lost their kiwis with kiwis bred in captivity. (Notice that as applied to this kind of restorative caring-for − 'justice towards', one might say − the forest or its population of kiwis, 'conservation' is, strictly speaking, an inaccurate description since there is nothing left to conserve.)

4. An example of the first kind of active caring-for earth might be drawn from gardening. (Heidegger observes (BDT p. 148) that though the discussion in 'Building Dwelling Thinking' is confined to the topic of 'construction', '*bauen*' (to build) really means not only 'to construct' but also 'to cultivate'. (One speaks in German of a '*Weinbau*', vineyard, a farmer is a '*Bauer*'.) The following might, therefore, be thought of as a contribution towards a 'second part' of that essay.)

Passive caring-for the earth is, of course, a central part of authentic gardening. As a dweller in a holy world, the authentic gardener will reverence the fundamental order of things already present in the site that is to be the garden rather than seeking to bulldoze a novel order. She will seek to 'tread lightly' on the site. Sometimes, however, her care for the site will be active rather than passive. Under what conditions? The *Sakutei-ki*, the classic, eleventh-century manual of Japanese gardening tells us that when constructing a garden we are to 'listen to the request made by the land'.[2] This is advice that will be followed by the authentic gardener. The 'request' may, for example, be for a lake. A correctly designed, planted and positioned lake may 'bring forth' the local birdlife, and in virtue of the serenity of its calm surface allow the contrasting 'stirring and striving' (BT 70) of the surrounding landscape to show forth in a more complete way. It also, of course, lets the contours of the landscape show forth by allowing them to repeat themselves in the mirror of its surface.

---

[2] See Gunter Nitschke's *Japanese Gardens* (Cologne: Benedikt Taschen, 1993) p. 57.

Both these aspects of gardening are, it seems to me, recorded in the first verse of Heidegger's 'Cézanne', a poem inspired by Cézanne's portrait of his gardener (see HPA chapter 4 section 19):

> The thoughtfully serene [*Gelassene*], the urgent [*inständig*]
> stillness of the form of the old gardener
> Vallier, who tends the inconspicuous on the
> *Chemin des Lauves*.   (D p. 163)

The old gardener's 'tending' is his passive caring-for the earth. And his 'urgent stillness' is, I suggest, an action-ready *listening* – a listening for and to 'the request made by the land'. (Notice the gardener's serenity, his *Gelassenheit* (see chapter 4 sections 3–5 above). As a dweller in a holy world he exhibits no anxiety in the face of his advanced mortality.)

5. Another example of active caring-for earth is 'organic' farming. Unlike farming which, as a branch of the 'mechanized food industry' (QCT p. 15), uses glass houses, artificial fertilizers and EU subsidies to compel the earth to yield whatever consumers demand, farming that actively cares-for the earth will be that which cultivates crops that bring forth the potentialities of the local soil, the *terroir* (both 'soil' and 'region'), as the French call it. Good vintners do this. One tastes the flint in the chardonnay.

6. Turning to architectural examples of, first, conservation of the earth, consider, to begin with, the 'motorway bridge [*Autobahnbrücke*]' which is 'tied into the network of long-distance traffic, placed as calculated for maximum speed' (BDT p. 152).[3]

'Building Dwelling Thinking' is, it seems to me, an attack on 'modernism' in the theory and practice of architecture, on the technology-deifying view which holds, in le Corbusier's slogan, that 'the house', buildings in general, are, and ought only to be, 'machines for living in'.[4] Alternatively put, it is

---

[3] Hofstadter's 'paced as calculated for maximum yield' – a comedy of typographical errors – makes no sense at all.

[4] Heidegger actually loved Corbusier, loved, at least, his chapel in Ronchamp, in Alsace, describing it as 'for the first time since the Gothic, a holy space' (E p. 136). The explanation of this seemingly paradoxical love for one of the leading propogandists of modernism lies in the fact that less than ten years after announcing the basic principles of what became known as the 'International Style' in his 1926 'Five Points of a New Architecture', Corbusier abandoned (or, at least, severely modified) those principles – forty years before most of the rest of the world began to question them. The outward sign of this abandonment was the replacement, in his later works,

an attack on the 'International Style', a style which is 'international' be-cause, fundamentally, the machine is international[5] – essentially the same whatever the context and locality in which it is to be used. The motorway bridge is Heidegger's paradigm of modernism: constructed solely according to 'long-distance' needs, it is the same wherever it is erected and so com-pletely insensitive to local considerations, to the site (fourfold) in which it finds itself. The motorway bridge violates its site.

So, usually, does the New Zealand farmhouse. Placed on its crest, it destroys the contour of the hill on which it is built. The Black Forest farmhouse, by contrast, conserves its landscape by being placed 'on . . . the mountain slope' (PLT p. 160); it is 'of' rather than 'on' the hill, to use Frank Lloyd Wright's distinction. Moreover, its 'wide overhanging shingle roof' is given its 'proper slope' (*ibid.*) so that it bears the weight of the snow and thereby obviates the need for the disruptive (and therefore ugly) presence of a protective retaining wall.[6] Further examples of passive caring-for earth might be Hundertwasser's grass-roofed, adobe-walled houses, Frank Lloyd Wright's low, strongly hor-izontal prairie houses which take care not to interrupt the flatness of the site, and his 'Falling Water' which, cantilevered over a waterfall, as its name says, allows the water to continue its fall.[7]

7. Heidegger's central illustration of active caring-for earth in architecture is 'the bridge'. Unlike the care-less vandalism of the motorway bridge,

---

of the machine-like forms and sleek finishes that were obligatory for modernism by, as in the case of the Ronchamp chapel, biomorphic contours and rough finishes.

[5] The modernist, mass-produced, 'you-can-have-any-colour-as-long-as-it-is-black' machine, at least. It is sometimes argued that, as we move into the 'postmodern' economy 'niche' pro-duction will replace mass-production, that we will move into a high-tec version of the craft economy. From a Heideggerian point of view such a transition might contain hopeful possibilities.

[6] As with Heidegger's hut at Totenauberg, a miniature version of the farmhouse, the Black Forest farmhouse is built, where possible, so that the sloping roof forms a lopsided V which collects snow and thereby insulates the house against 'the storms of long winter nights' (PLT p. 160).

[7] Frank Lloyd Wright strikes me as a wonderfully Heideggerian builder. He is, however, generally described as, in at least a broad sense, a modernist. The fact is, however, that, as applied to architecture, 'modernism' is ambiguous. Sometimes it is defined functionally – buildings ought to be machines for living and therefore 'International' in style – and sometimes formally – buildings ought to be devoid of ornament, have clean lines and form geometrical shapes. Wright, it seems to me, is a formal but certainly not a functional modernist. This makes the point (against the suggestion, sometimes made, that Heideggerian taste is confined to Black Forest kitsch) that Heidegger should by no means be regarded as being opposed to formal modernism. The Doric temple at Paestum he so much admired (OWA p. 40, pp. 41–3) is, after all, in *this* sense, a 'modernist' work.

Heidegger's authentic bridge – at this point its modelling on the so-called Old Bridge in Heidelberg[8] is clearly visible – is carefully placed so as to allow the river's 'banks' to emerge for the first time *as* banks rather than as mere 'strips' or edges. In doing this, says Heidegger, it gathers together 'earth as landscape' (BDT p. 152).

The point about 'banks' versus 'strips' is unity. Oceans do not have banks because their edges are not paired with one another. The dwelling architect, however, 'listening to the request' of the two landscapes to join (or rejoin) as one, 'completes' nature – 'the nature which "stirs and strives" . . . and enthralls us as landscape' (BT 70) – by bringing-forth what it itself 'strives' to achieve. In 'The Thing', Heidegger says, to repeat, that 'earth' itself 'builds', is the 'building bearer' (PLT p. 178). Authentic architecture is architecture which conserves and, as here, completes the earth's own building.[9]

Caring-for 'sky'

8. 'Sky', to repeat, is

the vaulting path of the sun, the course of the changing moon, the wandering glitter of the stars, the year's seasons and their changes, the light and dusk of day, the gloom and glow of night, the clemency and inclemency of the weather, the drifting clouds and blue depth of the aether.

Dwellers care-for 'sky', says Heidegger, when they

receive the sky as sky. They leave [*lassen*] to the sun and moon their journey, to the stars their courses, to the seasons their blessing and inclemency; they do not turn night into day nor day into harried unrest. (BDT p. 150)

'Sky', as Heidegger conceives it, seems to embrace, above all, the seasonal and diurnal rhythms, 'natural rhythms' as we called them in the 1960s. In the dweller's experience of nature as a holy place, these fundamental, structural features will be experienced as holy, too, as a 'quiet gift': this, for all its

---

[8] Though Medieval in style and referred to locally as 'the Old Bridge' it is, in fact, a nineteenth-century construction.

[9] Rory Spence has pointed out to me that Tomoya Masuda, professor of architecture at the University of Tokyo, who gave classes in the 1960s attended by visiting Europeans including the important Sydney architect, Richard Leplastrier, spoke about how traditional Japanese architecture helped to reveal the landscape: 'through architecture the landscape emerges'. Masuda also, it transpires, spoke at length about Heidegger.

hardness, is how the Black Forest peasant woman experiences the rhythms of her world in 'The Origin of the Work of Art''s celebrated rhapsody on van Gogh's painting of shoes (OWA p. 34).[10]

Experiencing his sky in this way, the dweller will wish to conserve the presencing of its holy rhythms. This might appear puzzling since (leaving aside the phenomenon of global warming) it might seem that we have *no option* but to 'leave . . . the seasons their blessing and inclemency' and so on. In Heidegger's picture, however, this is not the case. Seasonal and diurnal rhythms run as much through human as they do through natural phenomena. The farmer's planting is as much part of the onset of spring as is the thaw of ice, his harvesting as much the end of summer as the migration of the swallows.

The dweller will, therefore, wish to preserve the presencing of the holy rhythms in human life, in his own life and that of his fellows. He will wish to refrain from action which blocks the 'rece[ption] of sky as sky'. He will resist, for example, seven-day, twenty-four-hour shopping, the sixty-hour working-week, tradable holidays – holidays being, as we saw in chapter 3 (sections 20–22), special moments for 'coming to ourselves' and to the place in which we dwell. Accepting, enjoying, and communicating the enjoyment of the seasonality of fruit and vegetables might be another example of passively caring-for sky. Dwellers do not demand a round-the-year supply of avocados.

9. Is 'not turn[ing] day into night' a ban on electric lights, a symptom of Luddite techno-phobia? Does the presence of electric lights in Digne Meller Marcovitz's wonderful photographs of Heidegger's Black Forest hut[11] convict

---

[10] Heidegger may idealize peasant life, but his long and close personal knowledge of the exceptional hardness of attempting to farm the poor soil of the Black Forest means that it is far from sentimental. Though receiving 'the ripening of the grain' as nature's 'quiet gift', the peasant woman of the rhapsody also experiences 'anxiety as to the certainty of bread' and before the 'childbed'. Yet she endures these 'uncomplaining[ly]' (OWA p. 34). It is sometimes objected, particularly by Catholic theologians, that if the world is a holy place – if 'pantheism' is true, to resort for a moment to the inauthenticity of an 'ism' (LH p. 242) – then there is no room in it for the presence of evil nor, therefore, for the possibility of ethical endeavour. This, however, is a mistake. As the peasant woman understands, while the divinity of the world indeed entails the divinity of its fundamental order (what Hölderlin calls nature's underlying 'thought' (see chapter 3 footnote 2)), it in no way entails that everything in it is divine. The idea that the truly divine must be *flawlessly* divine is a prejudice of Christian theology I can see no reason to accept.

[11] See *Martin Heidegger: Photos 23 September 1966/16. und 17. Juni 1968* (Frankfurt-on-Main: Klostermann, 1985).

him of hypocrisy? Not so, for, as we have seen, the task is not to demonize technology – electricity, for example – but rather to learn to live with it, to incorporate it into a life of dwelling.

The passage in which Heidegger discusses 'receiving sky as sky' is, it needs again to be emphasized, highly *poetic*. It is intended, not to itemize the details of a twenty-point eco-plan for the active and passive care of climate, but rather to evoke the *Grundstimmung*, the 'fundamental mood' of dwelling. Understood poetically, 'not turning day into night' has clear application in a world *with* electricity. It might entail, for example, having e-mail only in one's office, leaving the cell-phone in one's car, not taking one's laptop away on holiday, searching for silence, in general preserving the rhythm of work and leisure.

In what might active caring-for, the 'bringing-forth' of, sky consist? Celebrating festivals such as the traditional wine and harvest festivals, perhaps. Farming and gardening with fitting, appropriate plants: plants such as the Chardonnay and Sauvignon Blanc grape which wonderfully express, not just the flinty 'earth' (*terroir*) of New Zealand's Marlborough region, but also, the 'marriage' in which 'the earth's nourishment and the sky's sun are betrothed to one another' (T p. 172). Ponds and lakes will be of interest to authentic gardeners as not only earth but also sky reflectors.

10. Turning to the conservation of sky in architecture we may note, first, that the modernist shopping centre is a depressing place in large part because it blocks out the ever-changing natural light and replaces it with, to borrow Heidegger's words, the 'monotonous and therefore oppressive' (QCT p. 17) uniformity of fluorescent light. Authentic builders will refrain from constructions which block in this way. Similar remarks apply to the blocking of the shifting vibrations of natural air. Authentic builders will, wherever possible, abhor the uniformity of air-conditioning.

Rather, and here we turn from passive to active caring-for sky in building, they will be disposed to replace fluorescent lights with skylights[12] and, even better, to construct open courtyards and perhaps a market place within the

---

[12] Notice that one and the same construction decision – the building of skylights – may simultaneously be both passive and active caring-for sky, both conservation and 'bringing forth'.

A particularly good example of the authentic use of skylights is provided by the work of Alvar Aalto. Aalto's prolific use of roof lighting is of particular significance in his native Finland where he was designing for a climate in which, for much of the year, it is difficult to be outside, under the sky.

mall. To allow for the circulation or real air, roofing will be kept to the minimum necessary to enable shoppers to shop even in bad weather.

Heidegger points out that the Black Forest farmhouse is situated on the mountain slope 'looking south', in other words, towards 'the sun and . . . [its] journey' (BDT p. 150). Other examples of actively bringing 'sky' into building might be: situating bedrooms and, as it used to be called, a 'morning room' facing East, towards the rising sun, and a living room facing West, towards its setting.

With respect to the authentic bridge, Heidegger seems to suggest that its being 'ready for the sky's weather and its fickle nature' (BDT p. 152) is an aspect of its 'bringing-forth' of sky. This is puzzling since one would think that *any* bridge – the inauthentic motorway bridge, too – has to be thus 'ready'. The point, however (one that is *not* especially well illustrated by the Heidelberg bridge), might be the following. A construction can be 'ready' for the climatic conditions inherent in its site either *brutally* – in virtue of the brute power of reinforced concrete – or else through the elegant use of minimal force. But minimal force technology is expressive. A bridge constructed as a thoughtful rather than forceful response to the local weather *expresses* that weather. This, perhaps, is why suspension bridges are often so beautiful. They are, as it were, wind harps, instruments which allow the wind to sing its song.

Caring-for 'gods'

11. Heidegger turns to caring-for gods in the following passage:

Mortals dwell in that they await the divinities as divinities. In hope they hold up to the divinities the unhoped-for (*das Unverhoffte*). They wait for intimations of their coming and do not mistake the signs of their absence. They do not make their gods and do not worship idols. In the very depth of misfortune they wait for the weal that has been withdrawn. (BDT p. 150)

The first puzzle presented by this enigmatic passage is: since modernity is the age of the absence of the gods, how is it possible for us to care-for them in any way at all? How can you care-for beings that are not there?

The solution to this puzzle is to remember (from chapter 7 section 6) that absence is 'not nothing' but rather 'unappropriated presence'. As heritage, the gods are always present. They are, however, pallid, sickly. They exist in a kind of *Götterdämmerung*, a twilight state. Since the role of a god is to 'dispose history', to be appropriated into the life of the community whose god it is, the gods do not, in the present age, flourish. To care-for the gods is, therefore, passively and actively, to promote their flourishing, their appropriation.

The passive caring-for on which Heidegger focuses is refraining from *manufacturing* gods, 'idols' that is to say. Dwellers 'do not make their gods for themselves'. It is impossible to doubt that the central reference of this 1951 remark is to Hitler. With this in mind, two questions need to be asked. Why are manufactured gods always fake gods, and, secondly, why is refraining from idolatry caring-for the true gods?

The answer to the first question is that since we do not need new gods – the true gods are already present 'in the divine in the world of the Greeks, in prophetic Judaism, in the preaching of Jesus' – manufactured gods are bound to be fake gods. The task is not to manufacture new gods but, rather, in the manner of *techne*, to 'bring forth' the ones that already exist, if only obscurely, in the life of the community. Dwellers, to repeat the remark from 'What are Poets for?', 'accomplish' but do not 'manufacture' (WPF p. 120).[13]

The answer to the second question is that since, as we know, the holy is the 'aether' in which alone gods can dwell (WPF p. 94), if we fill up the heart's space with a fake god no room is left in which the true gods can find an 'abode'. Caring-for of this sort is like the winter gardener's caring-for the coming of the plants of spring by keeping the ground free of weeds. Refraining from idol worship is a kind of spiritual 'weeding'. (In line with this is Heidegger's frequent observation that Nietzsche – the iconoclast – was no 'a-theist', that he was closer to God than many a so-called theist.)

12. Active caring-for the gods is, the passage says, 'wait[ing] for intimations'.[14] The important point to notice, here, is that Heideggerian 'waiting' is something completely different from apathy and inaction. It is, rather, 'guardianship . . . vigilance, watchfulness for the . . . coming destiny of

[13] The sixty-four-thousand dollar question is, of course: how is one to tell what is 'accomplished' and what 'manufactured'? As already remarked, there is, on Heidegger's view, no algorithmic procedure for answering this question. Since 'dissembling' is intrinsic to it (OWA p. 54), life is always a 'risk'. All one can do is to try to determine, to the best of one's ability, whether a putative god, a charismatic figure, is an embodiment of our fundamental 'heritage' or whether it is a fraud.

[14] The term 'intimation' is taken from Hölderlin (see HPA p. 114).

B/being' (PLT p. 184). Heideggerian waiting-for is, we might say, a waiting-on, a searching out and cultivation – 'bringing-forth' – of signs of the return of the gods.

In what might such waiting-on consist? Part of the task, we may speculate, could be assigned to artists. At one point Nietzsche writes that the task of the artist is to dedicate his powers

> not so much to the representation of the contemporary world or to the re-animation and imaginative reconstruction of the past, but to signposting the future – not, though, as if the poet could, like a fabulous economist, figuratively anticipate the kind of conditions nations and societies would prosper better under and how they could then be brought about. What he will do, rather, is to emulate the artists of earlier times who imaginatively developed the existing images of the gods and [thereby] *imaginatively develop* a beautiful image of man: he will scent out those cases in which, in the *midst* of our modern world and reality and without any artificial withdrawal from or warding off of this world, the great and beautiful soul is possible.[15]

In some ways unsurprisingly – since, as pointed out earlier, Heidegger's concept of a god is, in part, a development of Nietzsche's concept of a role-(or better, life-) model – this seems to embody the Heideggerian notion of cultivating the return of the gods. An historical example of this 'signposting' type of art is Socialist Realism, the idealization of farmers and workers in, perhaps, early Soviet iconography or in the works of Diego Rivera.

Another instance of such cultivation might be Pope John Paul II's watchfulness for the development of local cults of authentically saintly figures and his enthusiasm for beatifying and canonizing the objects of such cults. (The suspicion, however, that a right-wing political agenda colours and biases his activities, in other words that 'manufacture' rather than 'bringing forth' is the appropriate overall description of his beatifications, taints this example.)[16]

---

[15] *Human, all too Human*, Trans. R. J. Hollingdale (Cambridge: Cambridge University Press, 1986) pp. 235–6.

[16] The alert reader will notice that the above reading of Heidegger's account of caring-for the gods makes no reference to the second sentence of the passage: 'In hope they [those who care-for the gods] hold up to the divinities the unhoped-for [*das Unverhoffte*].' A possible reading of this extraordinarily obscure sentence might be the following. While the passage as a whole concerns the fostering of the appropriation of the gods by the community at large from which they are, at present, 'absent', the sentence in question concerns him to whom the gods are already present, namely, the dweller himself. His (active) caring-for the gods is a matter of his 'holding up' his life to them 'in the hope' that, grasped in the totality of its past, present and future, it may be worthy of the ideals of heritage which they personify. What he holds up is, perhaps, 'unhoped for' in the sense of '*otherwise* unhoped for'. Without the charismatic and so inspirational paradigms that the gods are, there would be no possibility of living a life that is consistently, 'resolutely' (OWA p. 67), worthy of them.

13. Turning to passive caring-for the gods in building, the extension of the above reflections is relatively obvious. Since caring-for the (true) gods entails refraining from worshipping false idols such as Hitler, caring-for them in building will consist, for example, in refraining from building monuments to fascist idols.

Heidegger's examples of active caring-for the gods in building – the figure of the saint on the old South German bridge (BDT p. 153), the '*Herrgottswinkel* [altar corner]' (BDT p. 160) in the Black Forest farmhouse – are both taken from times and places in which the gods are 'appropriated' by the culture as a whole. What, however, constitutes actively building for the gods, for their appropriation, in the age of their absence? Building shrines for those exceptional local communities in which, in contrast to the overwhelmingly godless character of modernity as a whole, worship of gods and saints still thrives, or is once more beginning to thrive, would be one example. Heidegger, however, focuses on something else.

Heidegger says, following Hölderlin, that the 'default' of the gods is due to the absence of 'holy names' (GA 4 pp. 27–8). Given Heidegger's understanding of absence as unappropriated presence, this should be taken to mean that we lack, not 'holy *names*' but, rather, '*holy* names'. The names of the divinities are known to us (preserved as 'heritage') but their bearers are 'absent' because, due to the loss of our sense of the sacred, such names have lost their 'radiance', are no longer *charismatic*. Given this diagnosis, the task of the architect, as it bears on godless modernity as a whole, is clear: to build spaces which are, like Corbusier's chapel at Ronchamp, 'holy spaces' (see footnote 4 above), spaces that foster the regrowth of the atrophied wings of the soul. Like every other artist of good times or bad, his task is to 'found the holy' (GA 52 p. 193, I p. 138, GA 4 p. 148).

Mindful of the omnipresence of the gods as heritage, Heidegger says that every bridge, even the motorway bridge, is a 'passage that crosses before the divinities – whether we explicitly think of, and visibly *give thanks for*, their presence, as in the figure of the saint on the bridge, or whether their presence is obstructed or even pushed entirely aside' (BDT p. 153) as by the motorway bridge.

Every human activity, every human construction, occurs 'before' the gods considered as heritage. A bridge, however, comes 'closer' to the gods than most other constructions since, in its 'vaulting' (BDT p. 153), it is an occasion for reflection upon, a natural metaphor for, men's 'striving to surmount all that is ordinary [*gewöhnlich*] and unsound [*unheil*] in them, in order to bring themselves before the haleness [*Heil*] of the divinities' (*ibid.*).[17] Every bridge, Heidegger suggests, is, potentially, a holy place.

The reason, I think, is that on a bridge one is raised above the 'harassed unrest' (BDT p. 150) of everyday life as it rushes onward beneath one's feet. It is natural to pause on a bridge, to take 'time out' for 'coming to oneself' ('festive' time). A bridge is a natural occasion for 'in hope hold[ing] up [one's life] to the divinities' (*ibid.*), for rededicating one's life, grasped as a whole, to the foundational values constitutive of one's heritage.[18] The motorway bridge, as itself a place of 'harassed unrest', misses out on, fails to 'bring-forth', this potentiality inherent in every bridge.

Could any *motorway* bridge bring-forth that potentiality, become an occasion for 'appropriating the gods' in the manner Heidegger envisages? The answer, I think, is that it could. Imagine, for example, not just a bridge over a motorway but a bridge to which is attached a resting place; not the usual McDonaldized crassness, but rather something somewhat like the wonderful Mövenpicks one finds in parts of Switzerland, a genuine resting place complete, let us say, with a garden, a pool, a fountain and perhaps a Matisse-designed, non-denominational chapel, a place for meditation.

On a more modest scale, on, say, a bridge over a river, the authentic builder would be disposed to build, in addition to footpaths, little spaces in which one might pause to stand and be transfigured. The (not-at-all-new) *Pont Neuf* in Paris, and, interestingly, the (not-at-all-old) Old Bridge in Heidelberg have just such spaces projecting out from the footpaths over the water.[19]

Caring-for 'mortals'

14. To care-for mortals is, says, Heidegger, to

escort [*geleiten*] their own nature – their being capable of death as death – into the use and practice of this capacity, so that there may be a good death. To initiate mortals into the nature of death in no way means to make death as empty nothing, the goal. Nor does it mean to darken dwelling by blindly staring toward the end. (BDT p. 151)

---

[17] Notice, in support of my account of Heidegger's gods as personifications of ethical perfection, that they are here said to be paradigms of ethical 'health'.

[18] In *Being and Time* it is in 'anticipation' of death that one grasps ones life as a 'totality' and becomes aware of its overall ethical character. The moment on the bridge is also, as we will shortly see, closely connected with death.

[19] Also the foot and cycle bridge opened over the Tyne in Newcastle, England, in 2001.

Human beings have, obviously, many important needs other than that of coming to terms with their own mortality. Heidegger is concerned here, however, with caring-for them specifically *as mortals,* as beings conscious of their own mortality. (Animals, though mortal, are not *mortals* because they are not conscious of the fact.) Characteristically, as already discussed (in chapter 4 section 3), we repress the knowledge of our own mortality and as a consequence live lives that are riddled with anxiety. Our primary spiritual need, therefore, is to become at home in our own 'nature', to overcome fear and anxiety in the face of death and so become capable of 'the good death'.

In what might passively caring-for mortals in their mortality consist? What is it, passively, to 'let death be' in our lives? Importantly, I would suggest, it consists in refraining from blocking the natural intrusions of death into life: in refraining from all of the death-evading 'idle talk' detailed in *Being and Time*, refraining from euphemisms about death, from face-lifts, from, probably, the embalming of corpses, and from anything that contributes to the 'professionalization' of death. Since mortals cannot be 'initiated' into its true and unfrightening nature unless death is allowed to be seen – to become a 'topic' – conserving the natural appearances of death in life is a necessary precondition for such an initiation.

Active caring-for mortals in their mortality, actively 'letting death be', might consist in making it into an emphatic, cathartic and affirmative ritual: the Maori *tangi*, for example, the celebration of a rite of passage common in non-Western cultures but, in the main, lost to Europeans. Most importantly, however, actively bringing forth the true nature of death is what is achieved by the 'meditative' and 'poetic thinking' we examined in chapter 4, thinking which, by overcoming metaphysics (the *empty* nothing), allows us to identify our true 'Selves', not with the mortal 'ego' but with, rather, the 'infinite totality' of Being itself.

15. How might architecture passively care-for mortals in their mortality? How might one, in one's practices as a builder, conserve the natural appearances of death in life? First and foremost, by not building Auschwitz, a place where, instead of *dying*, people 'are liquidated inconspicuously' as 'mere quanta, items in an inventory in the business of manufacturing

corpses'.[20] Other evasions of death the authentic builder is likely to avoid are, to repeat, old people's homes, which remove aging and death from the family's experience, and crematoria.[21] In general, the authentic builder will avoid anything that contributes to the 'mechanization' of death.

Active caring-for mortals in their mortality might consist in the building of tombs, gravestones and war memorials. Heidegger's own example is the inclusion in the design of the Black Forest farmhouse of a place not only for child-bearing but also for the coffin. In this way, says Heidegger, the house recalled for 'the different generations under one roof the shape of their journey through time' (BDT p. 160).

Returning to the authentic bridge, Heidegger suggests it to be a natural moment for, not only reviewing one's life as a totality in the light of heritage, but also for meditating on death: one's crossing of the bridge is a moment apt for reflection on one's last crossing, 'the last bridge' (BDT p. 153). This is no accidental conjunction. For, as *Being and Time* points out, since life becomes a totality only at the point of death, grasping it in its totality *is* grasping one's death. So the chapel or garden at the motorway bridge's resting place and Corbusier's 'holy space' will serve as places for 'time out'; for meditation on, not only the 'hale' in life, but also the mysterious yet unfrightening nature of death.

16. In the 'Letter on Humanism' Heidegger confronts and rebuts the accusation that *Being and Time* is a work of 'ontology' at the expense of 'ethics'. Properly thought out, he argues, ontology *is* ethics (LH pp. 268–71). In this chapter I have tried to demonstrate something similar with respect to later Heidegger. To adopt – adopt in life as well as the lecture-theatre – a proper relation to Being and truth, to overcome the tyranny of *Gestell* and the illusion of metaphysics, to become, in other words, one who dwells, is to understand a great deal about how one is to act or, at least, about how one is to

---

[20] This comes from an unpublished 1949 lecture called '*Die Gefahr*'. Cited in Thomas Sheehan's 'Heidegger and the Nazis', *New York Review of Books*, 16 June 1988, pp. 38–47. For a detailed discussion see HPN chapter 6 sections 1–8.

[21] Rory Spence has pointed out to me that in Scandinavia there is a strong tradition of seeking to design crematoria that avoid the industrialization of death. Alvar Aalto thought about the problem as, in Sweden, did Gunnar Asplund and Sigurd Lewerentz. The latter introduced the idea of leaving the chapel of the crematorium by a route different to that of one's arrival, so as to engender a more conscious sense of a rite of passage, and acceptance of the passing of another life.

'ponder'[22] about how to act. It is, in short, to possess an ethics. As Heidegger puts it, 'he who truly knows what is, knows what he wills to do in the midst of what is' (OWA p. 67). 'Insight into that which is' (T p. 46) is an ethics of action.

What kind of ethics? Clearly, as already intimated, not an algorithm that will generate for every situation of practical choice a uniquely correct decision. Take, for example, the hydro-dam. The dam, we have supposed, is violent technology because it refuses to let a river be itself. But sometimes one might think that a modest damming and the lake it creates 'brings forth' and completes the mountainous landscape in the way in which the pond in the Japanese garden completes its landscape. Vandalism or completion? Different 'ponderings of the dwelling-place' (see footnote 22 above) may come to different conclusions.[23] This, however, far from constituting a deficiency in Heideggerian ethics is, I would suggest, the nature of ethics as such. Ethics, that is to say, is riddled with indeterminacy (a realistic look at human history allows no other conclusion), situations in which the only hope of resolving ethical disputes is to seek to persuade the other to 'see' things in one's own way – to inhabit one's own *Gestalt* – in essentially the same way as one does in the case of aesthetic disputes. And as there is no guarantee of success in the latter case, neither is there in the former. Only someone blind to what Nietzsche called the 'tragic view' of life, someone captured by the Enlightenment illusion of the omnipotence of reason (an illusion which is itself part of *Gestell*) would suppose it to be possible for any ethics to generate a uniquely correct decision for every situation of practical choice.

17. A final comment on the ethics of dwelling. The reader will have noticed that many of the examples of active and passive caring-for the fourfold that I have proposed – saving forests, recycling waste, reducing pollution, living

---

[22] In the 'Letter on Humanism' Heidegger says, by way of a kind of definition, that 'ethics ponders [care-fully] the dwelling-place of human being' (LH p. 271).

[23] It might be thought that another indeterminacy is represented by, for example, the AIDS virus. Surely, it might be said, guardianship is guardianship of *every* natural species including (assuming that it *is* a natural species) the AIDS virus. But this is a misunderstanding. The object of guardianship is not each and every thing or kind of thing but, as we have seen, the fourfold, the dwelling-place as a whole. Since the virus threatens the elimination of one of its constituent elements, guardianship of the dwelling-place requires the elimination, or at least containment, of this threat. To generalize the point, guardianship of the dwelling-place sometimes calls for tough decisions with respect to some of its inhabitants, decisions in which the survival of the part may need to be sacrificed for the good of the whole.

in tune with 'natural rhythms', building locally rather than 'internationally' – represent practices we – some of us, that is – already engage in. This is quite deliberate. Unlike the Heidegger of 1934, thundering from the chilly and distant heights of Olympus and demanding the abolition of the world as we know it, later Heidegger is, in my view, *in* our world, an active participant and partisan in current debates. Partisan for what? For, in a word, 'ecological' thinking, though not in the usual sense in which 'ecology' means concern for non-human nature to the exclusion of everything else.

'Ecology' derives from the Greek '*oikos*' which means 'house' and 'house-keeping'. It is in this authentic sense of the word that Heidegger is, in my view, an 'ecological' thinker. He thinks, that is, towards care-taking the 'house', the house in which human beings – but human beings in inseparable[24] company with the creatures of earth, sky, and the holy 'aether' – dwell. 'Ethics', to repeat, 'ponders the dwelling place [the house] of human being'.

What is really important about Heidegger, however, is not that he has some attractive ideas about how we should take care of the dwelling-place. It is rather that these attractive ideas are *grounded*, grounded in his philosophy of B/being. The reason, to repeat, we should be 'guardians' of the 'house' lies not in human subjectivity – not in human interest, taste, or sentiment – but rather in the fact that, as a holy place, the 'house' *is* the to-be-cared-for. Heidegger's real achievement, therefore, is not to be an authentically ecological thinker, but to be the one, rather, who *founds* such thinking.

[24] 'Nature and history', to repeat, in their 'underlying and transcending of one another', 'interpenetrate' (AWP p. 129).

9   Fostering the growth of the saving Power

1. In chapter 6 I tabled the objection that Heidegger's later philosophy, while on close inspection not, in every respect, 'fatalistic' is nonetheless, in a bad sense, 'quietistic', a withdrawal from all action aimed at alleviating the 'destitution' of others. Immanuel Levinas has put this objection by suggesting that while the Heideggerian dweller is 'neighbour' to 'the Other' as Being, no such neighbourliness is displayed towards the Other as person.[1] Otherwise put, the charge is that the turn from Fascist activism to the alleged quietism of Heidegger's later philosophy is a turn from Fascism to a kind of self-absorbed navel-gazing, an 'inner emigration'. Thanks to the work of the last two chapters, we are now in a position to assess the weight of this criticism.

Love of the neighbour

2. Self-absorption is certainly not *intended* to be Heidegger's characterization of the dweller. Though he uses the word only sparingly – no doubt it sounds to him, as it did to Kant, too 'pathological', too closely tied to inner feeling – the salient characteristic in Heidegger's portrait of the dweller is, in fact, love, love, *contra* Levinas, for, above all, his fellow human beings.

In Hölderlin's 'Homecoming/to the Relatives', discussed by Heidegger in the essay of the same name (GA 4 pp. 9–31),[2] the poet descends from the Alps to the lake (Constance) on the further bank of which his 'relatives' (fellow Swabians and by extension Germans in general) live. High in the Alps he has had an epiphany, a direct encounter with, in Hölderlin's language, 'the Highest', 'the Joyful', and is in an ecstatic state. (In Heidegger's own language he has had the *'Ereignis*-experience', the experience of 'transport

---

[1] 'Is Ontology fundamental?' in *Philosophy Today*, vol. 33, 1989 pp. 121–8.
[2] With the possible exception of Sophocles, Hölderlin is the only thinker between whose voice and his own Heidegger allows no distance at all. When he says 'Hölderlin says . . .' he *always* means 'I say . . .'. See, further, HPA chapter 3.

and enchantment' (GA 65 p. 70).) The time, however, remains night and
something of the night attaches itself to the poet's mood. The reason is that
though, sensing always the closeness of Being (GA 4 pp. 54–5), he is never
lonely, he is, nonetheless, in a certain sense, alone. He is alone because the
'relatives', as still benighted, gods-less, are not yet properly related to him
(GA 4 p. 29). Because of this, and because his fundamental 'care' (GA 4
p. 28), as dweller and as poet, is that they should join him in the radiance of
the holy – that they, too, should dwell – his mood is tinged by sadness, a 'holy
mourning' (GA 39 *passim*) for the absence of the holy and of the gods. As here
portrayed, therefore, far from having abandoned 'the Other as person', the
dweller's primary care is for his fellows. Having made the turn to dwelling,
the dweller's primary care is that others should make that turning too.

Notice that this is no accidental niceness on the part of the dweller. Since,
along with the rest of the fourfold, our neighbours, our fellow 'mortals', show
up as holy beings, they show up as objects of love and care. The two modes
of 'caring-for mortals', as we saw in chapter 8, are an essential part of the
dweller's being-in-the-world.

Since, as Hölderlin sees, the primary 'plight' of modernity is 'homelessness', the dweller's primary care[3] is to relieve others of that primary 'misery'
(BDT p. 161). This requires that his primary activity should be, as *Being and
Time* in its own way saw, 'communication' (BT 384); communication of that
'insight into that which is' which overcomes metaphysics, allows 'releasement' from *Gestell* and from homelessness. Such communication may be
the communication of that which possesses 'might without force', namely,
'poetry and thought' (S p. 106), the kind of poeticizing and thinking which
'founds the holy'. It may take the form of Heidegger's own teaching and
writing (or of the writing of books such as this one which seek to pass on
Heideggerian insights). But it may also take the form of, in the widest sense of

---

[3] Primary care with respect to mortals but also, in a certain sense, primary care *überhaupt*.
Heidegger does not rank any element of the fourfold as more important, more care-worthy, than
any other. Since the fourfold is a 'simple oneness' (BDT p. 150), an organic unity in which
the intelligibility of any one element implies the intelligibility of all the others (see chapter 7
section 9 above), such a ranking would make no sense. The fact remains, nonetheless, that just
as the human being is the only possible 'guardian' of the fourfold, so he is its primary predator.
The only being who can 'save' the dwelling-place is also the being from whom it needs saving.
From this it follows that care for the dwelling-place must proceed, above all, *through* care for
mortals, and that in *this* sense, the dweller's care for mortals is prior to his care for the other
elements of the fourfold.

the word, 'building'; of building the kinds of buildings which, like Corbusier's chapel, found a 'holy space'. The fundamental importance of dwelling for building is, 'Building Dwelling Thinking' observes, that buildings built out of dwelling tend to 'let dwell', the fundamental goal of authentic architecture (BDT p. 146).[4]

Dwelling is, then, by no means self-absorption. The dweller's primary concern and activity is directed to fostering the dwelling of others. Heidegger, however, claims more for dwelling than this. When we as individuals 'look into the constellation of truth', he says, when, as individuals, we overcome metaphysics and make the turn to dwelling, 'we [collectively] are not yet saved'. The 'personal turning', as I have called it, is obviously neither the same as, nor entails, the 'world turning'. Nonetheless, the personal turning is not irrelevant to the world turning, for when we make it 'we [individually] are thereupon summoned . . . here and now and in little things [to] . . . foster the saving power in its increase' (QCT p. 33). To make the personal turning is, *ceteris paribus*,[5] to 'foster' the world turning. Why should this be so? Care for one's neighbour, communication of 'insight', is inevitably small-scale and localized. Unlike the impatient and grandiose plans of the mid-1930s for an overnight transformation of world-history through an alliance between 'poet' (Hölderlin), 'thinker' (Heidegger) and 'state-founder' (Hitler) (GA 39 p. 144), caring for one's neighbour through communication of insight is action on a modest scale, a dealing in 'little things'. Why, then, we must ask, should anything so modest be capable of promoting anything as grand as the world turning? Why should local action be capable of global consequences?

Cells of resistance

Let us remind ourselves of what it is that constitutes the world turning. It consists in the 'return of the gods', that is to say, their reappropriation by the community as a whole. Otherwise put, the world turning completes itself only when 'the artwork', in the sense deployed in 'The Origin of the Work of Art', only when 'the festival', returns. Only when individuals freely

---

[4] Buildings built out of dwelling are, of course, buildings built out of 'thinking' (BDT pp. 160–1): 'poetry . . . is the primal form of building' (PMD p. 227).
[5] Obviously the best laid plans can go astray. The dweller seeks, to the best of her ability, to promote the world turning, but she is not infallible.

gather in festal celebration of their communal gods, only, that is (GA 39 p. 216), when authentic community returns, has the world turning completed itself.

Why, then, to repeat the question, should my communication of metaphysics-overcoming insight to my neighbour promote anything as 'world-historical' as this?

Like every other human endeavour, Heidegger says in the *Spiegel* interview, philosophy is incapable of making history happen. Nonetheless it can have an 'indirect . . . effectiveness'. Though it cannot have a 'direct' effect on society at large – the dream of the Nazi Heidegger *den Führer zu führen* (to lead the leader) was the attempt at such a direct effect – a 'mediated effect' remains possible (S pp. 107–8). This repeats an observation made thirty years earlier in the *Introduction to Metaphysics*. Genuine philosophy, Heidegger realizes there, is 'essentially untimely'. It can never 'find an immediate echo in the present', 'can never directly supply the energies that create the opportunities and methods that bring about an historical change'. Nonetheless it is far from 'useless'. It can 'initiate profound transformations' which, however, 'spread only indirectly by devious paths which can never be laid out in advance'. Epochal historical change happens

only when an authentic knowledge of things dominates man's existence. And it is philosophy [and, later Heidegger would add, poetry] that opens up the paths and perspectives of such knowledge. (IM pp. 8–11)

Local communicative action can, therefore, Heidegger claims, 'in ways that cannot be laid out in advance', have global consequences.

The point is this. Though historical epochs are defined by a dominant mode of world-disclosure they are, as already observed, never homogeneous. In history,

there is never a mere sequence of things one after another: now *Gestell*, then world [i.e. fourfold] and thing; rather, there is always a passing by and simultaneity of early and late. (T pp. 184–5)

The historical epochs of a culture are, that is to say, always complex. They contain, always, a mainstream world-interpretation that defines the epoch (*Being and Time*'s 'the One [*das Man*]') but also individuals and sub-communities which swim in a different direction in that they represent either anticipations of future states of the culture or remnants of past states. An example of the latter is Christianity. Though we live in the age of 'the default of God' this 'does not deny that the Christian relationship with God lives on in individuals and in churches; still less does it assess this relationship negatively' (WPF p. 91). Examples of the former might be tramping clubs, 'Forest and Bird' societies, European ashrams, 'eco-villages', Celtic spiritualists, 'New Ageists' in general (though there is, of course, a great deal of the sham and sentimental in the New Age movement).

In sum, then, as with every culture, Western modernity resembles a river. In the centre of the stream is the main current. But at the edges are small eddies and tributaries which move at a different pace and sometimes in a contrary direction. Like every culture it is composed of the many who live in the mainstream and the few who live at the margins or, as Heidegger once put it, on 'reservations'.[6] (As *Being and Time* points out, through its not-so-idle 'idle talk', the mainstream always exerts tremendous pressure on the margins towards reintegration. The lives of those who swim against the current are not merely marginal but also marginalized, are held up as quaint, senseless, weird, or downright anti-social and dangerous.)

To make the personal turn to dwelling is, in modernity, to become 'untimely', voluntarily marginalized. Hence, though it should by now be clear that the personal turning is no 'inner' emigration, it *is* an 'emigration'. To make the turn is to become, as I should like to put it, a 'cell of resistance', resistance to *Gestell*.

As we have seen, however, the dweller's primary care is that others, too, should become dwellers. Dwellers are, therefore, cells of resistance which seek to create other cells of resistance which, in turn, seek to create still further cells. When her world shows up as a fourfold to the newly turned individual, her homeless fellows show up as to-be-relieved-of-their-'misery'. Dwelling, that is to say, has an infectious quality to it. It resembles a virus. This is the reason why the personal turn to dwelling is also a 'fostering' of the world's turning towards a new age. And it is also why Heideggerian thinking has always – absolutely correctly – been regarded as subversive by those locked into the mainstream of contemporary Western culture and philosophy.

---

[6] 'Today', he said, 'authentic thinking which explores the primordial lore of Being still lives only on "reservations"'. Quoted in O. Pöggeler, *Martin Heidegger's Path of Thinking* trans. D. Murgushak and S. Barber (Atlantic Highlands, NJ: Humanities Press, 1987) p. 191.

Of course, that you and I and those with whom we 'communicate' become dwellers is not the same as the return of the gods. But since the holy is the 'aether' in which alone gods can dwell (WPF p. 94), it is its essential precondition. By fostering the ever-widening shining of the 'divine radiance' (WPF p. 91) we foster, too, 'the saving power in its increase'.

Index